What Has Government Done to Our Money?

AND

The Case for a 100 Percent Gold Dollar

The Ludwig von Mises Institute dedicates this volume to all of its generous donors and wishes to thank these Patrons, in particular:

Dr. and Mrs. George G. Eddy

Douglas E. French and Deanna Forbush; John Hamilton Bolstad; Mr. and Mrs. Jeremy S. Davis; David Kramer; Roland Manarin; James M. Rodney; Mr. and Mrs. Edward Schoppe

Régis Alain Barbier; Toby Baxendale; Helio Beltrao; Richard Bleiberg; Herbert Borbe; Anthony Bouwman; Michael Todd Coakley; Carl Creager; Edward Dec; Raymond Delaforce; Dr. Larry J. Eshelman; Jon Ewigleben; Marc Faber; Stephen Fairfax; Karsten Franke; Henry Getz; Kevin Griffin; John A. Halter; Charles F. Hanes; Albert L. Hillman; Adam Hogan; Nicholas Jackson; Mr. and Mrs. Jason Jewell; Jonathan Liem; Arthur L. Loeb; Björn Lundahl; Frederick L. Maier; Mr. and Mrs. William W. Massey, Jr.; In Honor of Mikaelah and Ezra Medrano; Joseph Edward Paul Melville; Morgan Poliquin; Mr. and Mrs. Wilfried A. Puscher; Michael Robb; Mr. and Mrs. Joseph P. Schirrick; Lee Schneider; Conrad Schneiker; John Skar; Geb Sommer; Byron L. Stoeser; Markku Tuovinen; Frank Van Dun; Lawrence Van Someren, Sr.; Mr. and Mrs. Quinten E. Ward; Jim W. Welch; Dr. Thomas Wenck; Walter Wylie; Robert S. Young

WHAT HAS GOVERNMENT DONE TO OUR MONEY?

AND

THE CASE FOR A 100 PERCENT GOLD DOLLAR

MURRAY N. ROTHBARD

Ludwig
von Mises
Institute

AUBURN, ALABAMA

Published by Ludwig von Mises Institute, 518 West Magnolia Avenue, Auburn, Alabama 36832.

ISBN: 0-945466-44-7

Contents

What Has Government Done to Our Money?

THE CASE FOR A 100 PERCENT GOLD DOLLAR

WHAT HAS GOVERNMENT DONE TO OUR MONEY?

Preface to Fifth Edition

It has been said that the time of universal scholars ended long ago. There can be no more brilliant minds that develop vast systems of thought and produce top quality work across a range of disciplines. For such thinkers, we are told, there is neither supply nor demand.

The life and work of Murray Newton Rothbard (1926–1995) belies that rule. His more than twenty books, and literally thousands of book and magazine contributions, show that he had no equal as an economist, historian, political philosopher, and cultural critic. The enduring power of his thought makes it all the more necessary to read and learn from him today.

As an economist Rothbard stood in the tradition of the Austrian School, which was founded by Carl Menger and developed later by Eugen von Böhm-Bawerk and Ludwig von Mises. Rothbard made important contributions to the theory of monopoly, production, monetary, and welfare theory, among many other areas. His treatise *Man, Economy, and State* is a brilliant synthesis of his newer contributions and pre-existing theory.[1]

As a political philosopher, Rothbard provided a new foundation to the theory of human liberty by showing that the private ownership of property can serve as the basis of a comprehensive political ethics: the ethics of liberty.[2] This ethical foundation for liberty has a huge range of applications, even in areas in which it is traditionally said that the private sector is inadequate. Rothbard argued convincingly that a free society needs law and order, but not a state. Police and court services can and should be private, provided by associations and companies operating in the market economy on the basis of contract.

As a historian, Rothbard reformulated the history of money and banking in the United States,[3] most notably as it concerned the Great Depression,[4] and he wrote a general

---

[1]*Man, Economy, and State: A Treatise on Economic Principles*, 2 vols. (Princeton, N.J.: D. Van Nostrand, 1962; Los Angeles: Nash Publishing, 1970; New York: New York University Press, 1979; Auburn, Ala.: Ludwig von Mises Institute, 1993; combined with *Power and Market* to form the Scholar's Edition, Auburn, Ala.: Ludwig von Mises Institute, 2004).

[2]*The Ethics of Liberty* (Atlantic Highlands, N.J.: Humanities Press, 1982; reissued with a new introduction by Hans-Hermann Hoppe [New York: New York University Press, 1998]).

[3]*A History of Money and Banking in the United States: The Colonial Era to World War II*, edited with an introduction by Joseph T. Salerno (Auburn, Ala.: Ludwig von Mises Institute, 2002).

[4]*America's Great Depression* (Princeton, N.J.: D. Van Nostrand, 1963; 2nd ed., Los Angeles: Nash Publishing, 1972; rev. ed., New York: New York University Press, 1975; New York: Richardson and Snyder, 1983; 5th ed., with an introduction by Paul Johnson [Auburn, Ala.: Ludwig von Mises Institute, 2000]).

treatment of American history beginning in the Colonial Era.[5]

His treatment of the origin of bureaucracy employed new historical methods to understand the ideological impetus behind the creation and growth of the modern state.[6] Posthumously, Rothbard demonstrated his grasp of the history of ideas with a masterful reconstruction of the history of economic thought.[7] Released in the year of his death, this two-volume endeavor received international acclaim.

It was very late in his life before Rothbard's unique contribution to these many areas gained wide acknowledgment. The native New Yorker did not hold a prestigious chair at an American elite university. His radical views on theory, history, and policy rendered unattainable the Nobel Prize in economics which he deserved. Only at the age of 59 did he receive a position at a university of note (the University of Nevada, Las Vegas), which he held for the last ten years of his life.

That Rothbard managed to acquire an international reputation, and that his ideas had developed such a following in his lifetime, is due not to his status, position, or wealth but entirely to the strength of his arguments. When he died in 1995 at the age of 68, many of his works already appeared in foreign translations. Rothbard's contributions were featured in special issues of the *Journal of Libertarian Studies*, the *Quarterly Journal of Austrian Economics*, and the

---

[5]*Conceived in Liberty* (New Rochelle, N.Y.: Arlington House, 1975, 1976, 1979; Auburn, Ala.: Ludwig von Mises Institute, 1999).

[6]"Bureaucracy and the Civil Service in the United States," *Journal of Libertarian Studies* 11, no. 2 (Summer 1995): 3–75.

[7]*An Austrian Perspective on the History of Thought*, 2 vols. (Brookfield, Vt.: Edward Elgar, 1999).

Journal des Economistes Etudes Humaines. An entire book of appreciations was published as *Murray N. Rothbard: In Memoriam.*[8]

In 1997, Rothbard's most important articles were collected and published in the prestigious *Economists of the Century* series, which is edited by historian of thought professor Mark Blaug.[9] His academic citations have increased since his death.[10]

His political and social criticism from the 1990s were collected in a single volume,[11] a scholar's edition of his main treatise on economics (united with its original ending) has appeared,[12] and a biography published.[13]

Rothbard's books carry all the marks of a scholar in the classical tradition. They are written in crystal-clear language, are relentless in their method and pace of argument, always concentrate on the central issues, and treat all questions with comprehensive knowledge of the relevant literature.

What Has Government Done to Our Money? is an outstanding example of Rothbard's creative mind at work.

---

[8]Auburn, Ala.: Ludwig von Mises Institute, 1996.

[9]*The Logic of Action One and Two* (Cheltenham, U.K.: Edward Elgar, 1997).

[10]"The Unstoppable Rothbard," Mises.org: http://www.mises.org/story/1708.

[11]*The Irrepressible Rothbard: The Rothbard-Rockwell Report Essays of Murray N. Rothbard*, Llewellyn H. Rockwell, Jr., ed. (Burlingame, Calif.: Center for Libertarian Studies, 2000).

[12]*Man, Economy, and State with Power and Market* (Auburn, Ala.: Ludwig von Mises Institute, 2004).

[13]Justin Raimondo, *An Enemy of the State: The Life of Murray N. Rothbard* (Amherst, N.Y.: Prometheus Books, 2000).

Since it was first published in 1963, it has appeared in four editions in English, and has been translated into many foreign languages. It has served as a primer on monetary theory for all its readers. In fact, it is probably the most brilliant introduction to monetary theory ever written, presenting both the foundation of monetary theory and exploring the role of the state in the degeneration of monetary system. The book is suitable not only for economists, but also for nonacademics and all people interested in the subject. It is, like all of Rothbard's works, a timeless and powerful statement. It leaves the reader with a completely new way to think about the relationship between money and state.

Here the elements and the functions of a free monetary system are presented with brevity and clarity. Rothbard shows, how and why gold and silver are used as money on the unhampered market. Money originates neither from social compact nor government edict, but as a market solution of the problems and costs associated with barter. All other tasks usually considered monetary duties of the state—from minting to the definition of the monetary units to the precise form money will take—are left to private entrepreneurs on the unhampered market.

Where is the place of the state in this picture? Doesn't the state have to guard our money? Doesn't it have to adjust the money supply and supervise the banks? Rothbard's answer to these questions is a clear no. Government intervention does not protect money at all but rather threatens its integrity. Government interference leads to more abuse and more instability than the free market would otherwise have tolerated. Instead of solving problems, intervention creates them. Instead of order they bring chaos and economic upheaval.

For Rothbard, the central issue is not whether monetary policy should stabilize the price level or the money supply; it is whether there is a role for the state in the monetary system at all. On this question, Rothbard answers decisively in the negative. Entrusting the money to the state is a grave error. It opens door and gate for totalitarian control of the society by interest groups closely connected to the state apparatus. The consequences are economic and monetary crises, and a relentless decline in purchasing power of money. Rothbard illustrates this impressively with a short history of the monetary collapse of the West.

Rothbard's chronicle of decline ends with the breakdown of Bretton Woods and a prediction that the future portends continued exchange-rate volatility, debt accumulation, inflation, crises, bailouts, and a political drive to further centralize control of money and credit. This prediction turned out to be a good summary of the monetary events of the last quarter century.[14] The world economy adopted a *de facto* dollar standard, a managed monetary integration came to Europe, and crisis has followed crisis in Asia, Russia, Mexico and Central and South America, along with exploding deficits and debts in the U.S. Undoubtedly many more will come our way.

This new edition includes a detailed reform proposal for a 100 percent gold dollar, an essay first published in 1962, the same year that *Man, Economy, and State* appeared and two years before *What Has Government Done to Our Money?* That it was written a decade before the last vestiges of the

---

[14]Many commentaries on subsequent events can be found in Murray N. Rothbard, *Making Economic Sense* (Auburn, Ala.: Ludwig von Mises Institute, 1995), pp. 253–301.

gold standard were abolished does not diminish its power as a proposal for reform.

Would Rothbard's plan work? Certainly. The limits are due not to its economic viability but rather to the same forces that keep all radical proposals for freedom at bay: political barriers and ideological opposition. Should the conditions ever become ripe for pure liberty again—and Rothbard was ever the optimist—this essay will serve as an outstanding blueprint.

Today all nations face a choice between sound money and continuing monetary depreciation and/or monetary crisis. Sound money, Rothbard shows, means the enforcement of strict separation between the state and money. Rothbard has shown that the world's party of liberty can embrace what is usually said to be an impossible ideal: an international money protected against the arbitrariness of the state. His analysis and prescriptions deserve even more attention today than when they were first written.

Jörg Guido Hülsmann
Angers, France
April 2005

I.

INTRODUCTION

FEW ECONOMIC SUBJECTS ARE more tangled, more confused than money. Wrangles abound over "tight money" vs. "easy money," over the roles of the Federal Reserve System and the Treasury, over various versions of the gold standard, etc. Should the government pump money into the economy or siphon it out? Which branch of the government? Should it encourage credit or restrain it? Should it return to the gold standard? If so, at what rate? These and countless other questions multiply, seemingly without end.

Perhaps the Babel of views on the money question stems from man's propensity to be "realistic," i.e., to study only immediate political and economic problems. If we immerse ourselves wholly in day-to-day affairs, we cease making fundamental distinctions, or asking the really basic questions. Soon, basic issues are forgotten, and aimless drift is substituted for firm adherence to principle. Often we need to gain perspective, to stand aside from our everyday

affairs in order to understand them more fully. This is particularly true in our economy, where interrelations are so
intricate that we must isolate a few important factors, analyze them, and then trace their operations in the complex
world. This was the point of "Crusoe economics," a favorite
device of classical economic theory. Analysis of Crusoe and
Friday on a desert island, much abused by critics as irrelevant to today's world, actually performed the very useful
function of spotlighting the basic axioms of human action.

Of all the economic problems, money is possibly the
most tangled, and perhaps where we most need perspective.
Money, moreover, is the economic area most encrusted and
entangled with centuries of government meddling. Many
people—many economists—usually devoted to the free
market stop short at money. Money, they insist, is different;
it must be supplied by government and regulated by government. They never think of state control of money as
interference in the free market; a free market in money is
unthinkable to them. Governments must mint coins, issue
paper, define "legal tender," create central banks, pump
money in and out, "stabilize the price level," etc.

Historically, money was one of the first things controlled by government, and the free market "revolution" of
the eighteenth and nineteenth centuries made very little
dent in the monetary sphere. So it is high time that we turn
fundamental attention to the life-blood of our economy—
money.

Let us first ask ourselves the question: *Can* money be
organized under the freedom principle? Can we have a
free market in money as well as in other goods and services? What would be the shape of such a market? And what
are the effects of various governmental controls? If we favor
the free market in other directions, if we wish to eliminate

government invasion of person and property, we have no more important task than to explore the ways and means of a free market in money.

II.
MONEY IN A FREE SOCIETY

1.
The Value of Exchange

HOW DID MONEY BEGIN? Clearly, Robinson Crusoe had no need for money. He could not have eaten gold coins. Neither would Crusoe and Friday, perhaps exchanging fish for lumber, need to bother about money. But when society expands beyond a few families, the stage is already set for the emergence of money.

To explain the role of money, we must go even further back, and ask: why do men exchange at all? Exchange is the prime basis of our economic life. Without exchanges, there would be no real economy and, practically, no society. Clearly, a voluntary exchange occurs because both parties expect to benefit. An exchange is an agreement between *A* and *B* to transfer the goods or services of one man for the goods and services of the other. Obviously, both benefit because each values what he receives in exchange more than what he gives up. When Crusoe, say, exchanges some fish for lumber, he values the lumber he "buys" more than

the fish he "sells," while Friday, on the contrary, values the
fish more than the lumber. From Aristotle to Marx, men
have mistakenly believed that an exchange records some
sort of equality of value—that if one barrel of fish is
exchanged for ten logs, there is some sort of underlying
equality between them. Actually, the exchange was made
only because each party valued the two products in *different*
order.

Why should exchange be so universal among mankind?
Fundamentally, because of the great *variety* in nature: the
variety in man, and the diversity of location of natural
resources. Every man has a different set of skills and apti-
tudes, and every plot of ground has its own unique features,
its own distinctive resources. From this external natural fact
of variety come exchanges; wheat in Kansas for iron in
Minnesota; one man's medical services for another's play-
ing of the violin. Specialization permits each man to
develop his best skill, and allows each region to develop its
own particular resources. If no one could exchange, if every
man were forced to be completely self-sufficient, it is obvious that most of us would starve to death, and the rest
would barely remain alive. Exchange is the lifeblood, not
only of our economy, but of civilization itself.

2.

Barter

Yet, *direct exchange* of useful goods and services would
barely suffice to keep an economy going above the primitive
level. Such direct exchange—or *barter*—is hardly better
than pure self-sufficiency. Why is this? For one thing, it is
clear that very little production could be carried on. If Jones
hires some laborers to build a house, with what will he pay

them? With parts of the house, or with building materials they could not use? The two basic problems are "indivisibility" and "lack of coincidence of wants." Thus, if Smith has a plow, which he would like to exchange for several different things—say, eggs, bread, and a suit of clothes—how can he do so? How can he break up the plow and give part of it to a farmer and another part to a tailor? Even where the goods are divisible, it is generally impossible for two exchangers to find each other at the same time. If *A* has a supply of eggs for sale, and *B* has a pair of shoes, how can they get together if *A* wants a suit? And think of the plight of an economics teacher who has to find an egg-producer who wants to purchase a few economics lessons in return for his eggs! Clearly, any sort of civilized economy is impossible under direct exchange.

3.
Indirect Exchange

But man discovered, in the process of trial and error, the route that permits a greatly-expanding economy: *indirect* exchange. Under indirect exchange, you sell your product not for a good which you need directly, but for another good which you then, in turn, sell for the good you want. At first glance, this seems like a clumsy and round-about operation. But it is actually the marvelous instrument that permits civilization to develop.

Consider the case of *A*, the farmer, who wants to buy the shoes made by *B*. Since *B* doesn't want his eggs, he finds what *B does* want—let's say butter. *A* then exchanges his eggs for C's butter, and sells the butter to *B* for shoes. He first buys the butter not because he wants it directly, but because it will permit him to get his shoes. Similarly, Smith, a plow-owner, will sell his plow for one commodity which he can more readily divide and sell—say, butter—and will then exchange parts of the butter for eggs, bread, clothes, etc. In both cases, the superiority of butter—the reason there is extra demand for it beyond simple consumption—is its greater *marketability*. If one good is more marketable than another—if everyone is confident that it will be more readily sold—then it will come into greater demand because it will be used as a *medium of exchange*. It will be the medium through which one specialist can exchange his product for the goods of other specialists.

Now just as in nature there is a great variety of skills and resources, so there is a variety in the marketability of goods. Some goods are more widely demanded than others, some are more divisible into smaller units without loss of value, some more durable over long periods of time, some more transportable over large distances. All of these advantages make for greater marketability. It is clear that in every society, the most marketable goods will be gradually selected as the media for exchange. As they are more and more selected as media, the demand for them increases because of this use, and so they become even more *marketable*. The result is a reinforcing spiral: more marketability causes wider use as a medium which causes more marketability, etc. Eventually, one or two commodities are used as general *media*—in almost all exchanges—and these are called money.

Historically, many different goods have been used as media: tobacco in colonial Virginia, sugar in the West Indies, salt in Abyssinia, cattle in ancient Greece, nails in Scotland, copper in ancient Egypt, and grain, beads, tea, cowrie shells, and fishhooks. Through the centuries, two commodities, *gold* and *silver*, have emerged as money in the free competition of the market, and have displaced the other commodities. Both are uniquely marketable, are in great demand as ornaments, and excel in the other necessary qualities. In recent times, silver, being relatively more abundant than gold, has been found more useful for smaller exchanges, while gold is more useful for larger transactions. At any rate, the important thing is that whatever the reason, the free market has found gold and silver to be the most efficient moneys.

This process: the cumulative development of a medium of exchange on the free market—is the only way money can become established. Money cannot originate in any other way, neither by everyone suddenly deciding to create money out of useless material, nor by government calling bits of paper "money." For embedded in the demand for money is knowledge of the money-prices of the immediate past; in contrast to directly-used consumers' or producers' goods, money must have preexisting prices on which to ground a demand. But the only way this can happen is by beginning with a useful commodity under barter, and then adding demand for a medium for exchange to the previous demand for direct use (e.g., for ornaments, in the case of gold).[1] Thus, government is powerless to create money for the economy; it can only be developed by the processes of the free market.

A most important truth about money now emerges from our discussion: money is a commodity. Learning this simple lesson is one of the world's most important tasks. So often have people talked about money as something much more or less than this. Money is not an abstract unit of account,

---

[1]On the origin of money, cf. Carl Menger, *Principles of Economics* (Glencoe, Ill.: Free Press, 1950), pp. 257–71; Ludwig von Mises, *The Theory of Money and Credit*, 3rd ed. (New Haven, Conn.: Yale University Press, 1951), pp. 97–123.

divorceable from a concrete good; it is not a useless token only good for exchanging; it is not a "claim on society"; it is not a guarantee of a fixed price level. It is simply a commodity. It differs from other commodities in being demanded mainly as a medium of exchange. But aside from this, it is a commodity—and, like all commodities, it has an existing stock, it faces demands by people to buy and hold it, etc. Like all commodities, its "price"—in terms of other goods—is determined by the interaction of its total supply, or stock, and the total demand by people to buy and hold it. (People "buy" money by selling their goods and services for it, just as they "sell" money when they buy goods and services.)

4.
Benefits of Money

The emergence of money was a great boon to the human race. Without money—without a general medium of exchange—there could be no real specialization, no advancement of the economy above a bare, primitive level. With money, the problems of indivisibility and "coincidence of wants" that plagued the barter society all vanish. Now, Jones can hire laborers and pay them in . . . money. Smith can sell his plow in exchange for units of . . . money. The money-commodity is divisible into small units, and it is generally acceptable by all. And so all goods and services are sold for money, and then money is used to buy other goods and services that people desire. Because of money, an elaborate "structure of production" can be formed, with land, labor services, and capital goods cooperating to advance production at each stage and receiving payment in money.

The establishment of money conveys another great benefit. Since all exchanges are made in money, all the exchange-ratios are expressed in money, and so people can now compare the market worth of each good to that of every other good. If a TV set exchanges for three ounces of gold, and an automobile exchanges for sixty ounces of gold, then everyone can see that one automobile is "worth" twenty TV sets on the market. These exchange-ratios are *prices*, and the money-commodity serves as a common denominator for all prices. Only the establishment of money-prices on the market allows the development of a civilized economy, for only they permit businessmen to *calculate* economically. Businessmen can now judge how well they are satisfying consumer demands by seeing how the selling-prices of their products compare with the prices they have to pay productive factors (their "costs"). Since all these prices are expressed in terms of money, the businessmen can determine whether they are making profits or losses. Such calculations guide businessmen, laborers, and landowners in their search for monetary income on the market. Only such calculations can allocate resources to their most productive uses—to those uses that will most satisfy the demands of consumers.

Many textbooks say that money has several functions: a medium of exchange, unit of account, or "measure of values," a "store of value," etc. But it should be clear that all of these functions are simply corollaries of the one great function: the medium of exchange. Because gold is a general medium, it is most marketable, it can be stored to serve as a medium in the future as well as the present, and all prices are expressed in its terms.[2] Because gold is a commodity medium for all exchanges, it can serve as a unit of

---

[2]Money does not "measure" prices or values; it is the common denominator for their expression. In short, prices are expressed in money; they are not measured by it.

account for present, and expected future, prices. It is important to realize that money cannot be an abstract unit of account or claim, except insofar as it serves as a medium of exchange.

5.
The Monetary Unit

Now that we have seen how money emerged, and what it does, we may ask: how is the money-commodity used? Specifically, what is the stock, or supply, of money in society, and how is it exchanged?

In the first place, most tangible physical goods are traded in terms of weight. Weight is the distinctive unit of a tangible commodity, and so trading takes place in terms of units like tons, pounds, ounces, grains, grams, etc.[3] Gold is no exception. Gold, like other commodities, will be traded in units of weight.[4]

It is obvious that the size of the common unit chosen in trading makes no difference to the economist. One country, on the metric system, may prefer to figure in grams; England or America may prefer to reckon in grains or ounces. All units of weight are convertible into each other; one pound equals sixteen ounces; one ounce equals 437.5 grains or 28.35 grams, etc.

---

[3]Even those goods nominally exchanging in terms of *volume* (bale, bushel, etc.) tacitly assume a standard weight per unit volume.

[4]One of the cardinal virtues of gold as money is its *homogeneity*—unlike many other commodities, it has no differences in quality. An ounce of pure gold equals any other ounce of pure gold the world over.

Assuming gold is chosen as the money, the size of the gold-unit used in reckoning is immaterial to us. Jones may sell a coat for one gold ounce in America, or for 28.35 grams in France; both prices are identical.

All this might seem like laboring the obvious, except that a great deal of misery in the world would have been avoided if people had fully realized these simple truths. Nearly everyone, for example, thinks of money as abstract units for something or other, each cleaving uniquely to a certain country. Even when countries were on the "gold standard," people thought in similar terms. American money was "dollars," French was "francs," German "marks," etc. All these were admittedly tied to gold, but all were considered sovereign and independent, and hence it was easy for countries to "go off the gold standard." *Yet all of these names were simply names for units of weight of gold or silver.*

The British "pound sterling" originally signified a pound weight of silver. And what of the dollar? The dollar began as the generally applied name of an ounce weight of silver coined by a Bohemian Count named Schlick, in the sixteenth century. The Count of Schlick lived in Joachim's Valley or Jaochimsthal. The Count's coins earned a great reputation for their uniformity and fineness, and they were widely called "Joachim's thalers," or, finally, "thaler." The name "dollar" eventually emerged from "thaler."

On the free market, then, the various names that units may have are simply *definitions of units of weight*. When we were "on the gold standard" before 1933, people liked to say that the "price of gold" was "fixed at twenty dollars per ounce of gold." But this was a dangerously misleading way of looking at our money. Actually, "the dollar" was *defined* as the *name for* (approximately) 1/20 of an ounce of gold. It was therefore misleading to talk about "exchange rates" of one country's currency for another. The "pound sterling" did not really "exchange" for five "dollars."[5] The dollar was defined as 1/20 of a gold ounce, and the pound sterling was, at that time, defined as the name for 1/4 of a gold ounce, simply traded for 5/20 of a gold ounce. Clearly, such exchanges, and such a welter of names, were confusing and misleading. How they arose is shown below in the chapter on government meddling with money. In a purely free market, gold would simply be exchanged directly as "grams," grains, or ounces, and such confusing names as dollars, francs, etc., would be superfluous. Therefore, in this section, we will treat money as exchanging directly in terms of ounces or grams.

Clearly, the free market will choose as the common unit whatever size of the money-commodity is most convenient. If platinum were the money, it would likely be traded in terms of fractions of an ounce; if iron were used, it would be reckoned in pounds or tons. Clearly, the size makes no difference to the economist.

6.
The Shape of Money

If the size or the name of the money-unit makes little economic difference; neither does the shape of the monetary metal. Since the commodity is the money, it follows that the *entire* stock of the metal, so long as it is available to

---

[5]Actually, the pound sterling exchanged for $4.87, but we are using $5 for greater convenience of calculation.

man, constitutes the world's stock of money. It makes no
real difference what shape any of the metal is at any time. If
iron is the money, then *all* the iron is money, whether it is in
the form of bars, chunks, or embodied in specialized
machinery.[6] Gold has been traded as money in the raw form
of nuggets, as gold dust in sacks, and even as jewelry. It
should not be surprising that gold, or other moneys, can be
traded in many forms, since their important feature is their
weight.

It is true, however, that some shapes are often more convenient than others. In recent centuries, gold and silver
have been broken down into *coins*, for smaller, day-to-day
transactions, and into larger bars for bigger transactions.
Other gold is transformed into jewelry and other ornaments. Now, any kind of transformation from one shape to
another costs time, effort, and other resources. Doing this
work will be a business like any other, and prices for this
service will be set in the usual manner. Most people agree
that it is legitimate for jewelers to make ornaments out of
raw gold, but they often deny that the same applies to the
manufacture of coins. Yet, on the free market, coinage is
essentially a business like any other.

Many people believed, in the days of the gold standard,
that coins were somehow more "really" money than plain,
uncoined gold "bullion" (bars, ingots, or any other shape).
It is true that coins commanded a premium over bullion,
but this was not caused by any mysterious virtue in the
coins; it stemmed from the fact that it cost more to manufacture coins from bullion than to remelt coins back into

---

[6]Iron hoes have been used extensively as money, both in Asia and Africa.

bullion. Because of this difference, coins were more valuable on the market.

7.
Private Coinage

The idea of private coinage seems so strange today that it is worth examining carefully. We are used to thinking of coinage as a "necessity of sovereignty." Yet, after all, we are not wedded to a "royal prerogative," and it is the American concept that sovereignty rests, not in government, but in the people.

How would private coinage work? In the same way, we have said, as any other business. Each minter would produce whatever size or shape of coin is most pleasing to his customers. The price would be set by the free competition of the market.

The standard objection is that it would be too much trouble to weigh or assay bits of gold at every transaction. But what is there to prevent private minters from stamping the coin and guaranteeing its weight and fineness? Private minters can guarantee a coin at least as well as a government mint. Abraded bits of metal would not be accepted as coin. People would use the coins of those minters with the best reputation for good quality of product. We have seen that this is precisely how the "dollar" became prominent— as a competitive silver coin.

Opponents of private coinage charge that fraud would run rampant. Yet, these same opponents would trust government to provide the coinage. But if government is to be trusted at all, then surely, with private coinage, government could at least be trusted to prevent or punish fraud. It is usually assumed that the prevention or punishment of fraud, theft, or other crimes is the real justification for government. But if government cannot apprehend the criminal when private coinage is relied upon, what hope is there for a reliable coinage when the integrity of the private market place operators is discarded in favor of a government monopoly of coinage? If government cannot be trusted to ferret out the occasional villain in the free market in coin, why can government be trusted when it finds itself in a position of total control over money and may debase coin, counterfeit coin, or otherwise with full legal sanction perform as the sole villain in the market place? It is surely folly to say that government must socialize all property in order to prevent anyone from stealing property. Yet the reasoning behind abolition of private coinage is the same.

Moreover, all modern business is built on guarantees of standards. The drug store sells an eight ounce bottle of medicine; the meat packer sells a pound of beef. The buyer expects these guarantees to be accurate, and they are. And think of the thousands upon thousands of specialized, vital industrial products that must meet very narrow standards and specifications. The buyer of a 1/2 inch bolt must get a 1/2 inch bolt and not a mere 3/8 inch.

Yet, business has not broken down. Few people suggest that the government must nationalize the machine-tool industry as part of its job of defending standards against fraud. The modern market economy contains an infinite number of intricate exchanges, most depending on definite standards of quantity and quality. But fraud is at a minimum, and that minimum, at least in theory, may be prosecuted. So it would be if there were private coinage. We can be sure that a minter's customers, and his competitors, would be keenly alert to any possible fraud in the weight or fineness of his coins.[7]

Champions of the government's coinage monopoly have claimed that money is different from all other commodities, because "Gresham's Law" proves that "bad money drives out good" from circulation. Hence, the free market cannot be trusted to serve the public in supplying good money. But this formulation rests on a misinterpretation of Gresham's famous law. The law really says that "money overvalued artificially by government will drive out of circulation artificially undervalued money." Suppose, for example, there are one-ounce gold coins in circulation. After a few years of wear and tear, let us say that some coins weigh only .9 ounces. Obviously, on the free market, the worn coins would circulate at only 90 percent of the value of the full-bodied coins, and the nominal face-value of the former would have to be repudiated.[8] If anything, it will be the "bad" coins that will be driven from the market. But suppose the government decrees that everyone must treat the worn coins as equal to new, fresh coins, and must accept them equally in payment of debts. What has the government really done? It has imposed *price control* by coercion on the "exchange rate" between the two types of coin. By insisting on the par-ratio when the worn coins should exchange at 10 percent discount, it artificially *overvalues* the worn coins and *undervalues* new coins. Consequently,

---

[7]See Herbert Spencer, *Social Statics* (New York: D. Appleton 1890), p. 438.

[8]To meet the problem of wear-and-tear, private coiners might either set a time limit on their stamped guarantees of weight, or agree to recoin anew, either at the original or at the lower weight. We may note that in the free economy there will not be the compulsory standardization of coins that prevails when government monopolies direct the coinage.

everyone will circulate the worn coins, and hoard or export the new. "Bad money drives out good money," then, *not* on the free market, but as the direct result of governmental intervention in the market.

Despite never-ending harassment by governments, making conditions highly precarious, private coins have flourished many times in history. True to the virtual law that all innovations come from free individuals and not the state, the first coins were minted by private individuals and goldsmiths. In fact, when the government first began to monopolize the coinage, the royal coins bore the guarantees of private bankers, whom the public trusted far more, apparently, than they did the government. Privately-minted gold coins circulated in California as late as 1848.[9]

8.
The "Proper" Supply of Money

Now we may ask: what is the supply of money in society and how is that supply used? In particular, we may raise the perennial question, how much money "do we need"? Must the money supply be regulated by some sort of "criterion," or can it be left alone to the free market?

---

[9]For historical examples of private coinage, see B.W. Barnard, "The use of Private Tokens for Money in the United States," *Quarterly Journal of Economics* (1916–17): 617–26; Charles A. Conant, *The Principles of Money and Banking* (New York: Harper Bros., 1905), vol. I, 127–32; Lysander Spooner, *A Letter to Grover Cleveland* (Boston: B.R. Tucker, 1886), p. 79; and J. Laurence Laughlin, *A New Exposition of Money, Credit and Prices* (Chicago: University of Chicago Press, 1931), vol. I, pp. 47–51. On coinage, also see Mises, *Theory of Money and Credit*, pp. 65–67; and Edwin Cannan, *Money*, 8th ed. (London: Staples Press, 1935), pp. 33ff.

First, *the total stock, or supply, of money in society at any one time, is the total weight of the existing money-stuff.* Let us assume, for the time being, that only *one* commodity is established on the free market as money. Let us further assume that *gold* is that commodity (although we could have taken silver, or even iron; it is up to the *market*, and not to us, to decide the best commodity to use as money). Since money is gold, the total supply of money is the total weight of gold existing in society. The *shape* of gold does not matter—except if the cost of changing shapes in certain ways is greater than in others (e.g., minting coins costing more than melting them). In that case, one of the shapes will be chosen by the market as the money-of-account, and the other shapes will have a premium or discount in accordance with their relative costs on the market.

Changes in the total gold stock will be governed by the same causes as changes in other goods. Increases will stem from greater production from mines; decreases from being used up in wear and tear, in industry, etc. Because the market will choose a durable commodity as money, and because money is not used up at the rate of other commodities—but is employed as a medium of exchange—the proportion of new annual production to its total stock will tend to be quite small. Changes in total gold stock, then, generally take place very slowly.

What "should" the supply of money be? All sorts of criteria have been put forward: that money should move in accordance with population, with the "volume of trade," with the "amounts of goods produced," so as to keep the "price level" constant, etc. Few indeed have suggested leaving the decision to the market. But money differs from other commodities in one essential fact. And grasping this difference furnishes a key to understanding monetary matters.

When the supply of any other good increases, this increase confers a social benefit; it is a matter for general rejoicing. More consumer goods mean a higher standard of living for the public; more capital goods mean sustained and increased living standards in the future. The discovery of new, fertile land or natural resources also promises to add to living standards, present and future. But what about money? Does an addition to the money supply also benefit the public at large?

Consumer goods are used up by consumers; capital goods and natural resources are used up in the process of producing consumer goods. But money is not used up; its function is to act as a medium of exchanges—to enable goods and services to travel more expeditiously from one person to another. These exchanges are all made in terms of money prices. Thus, if a television set exchanges for three gold ounces, we say that the "price" of the television set is three ounces. At any one time, all goods in the economy will exchange at certain gold-ratios or prices. As we have said, money, or gold, is the common denominator of all prices. But what of money itself? Does it have a "price"? Since a price is simply an exchange-ratio, it clearly does. But, in this case, the "price of money" is an *array* of the infinite number of exchange-ratios for all the various goods on the market.

Thus, suppose that a television set costs three gold ounces, an auto sixty ounces, a loaf of bread 1/100 of an ounce, and an hour of Mr. Jones's legal services one ounce. The "price of money" will then be an array of alternative exchanges. One ounce of gold will be "worth" either 1/3 of a television set, 1/60 of an auto, 100 loaves of bread, or one hour of Jones's legal service. And so on down the line. The price of money, then, is the "purchasing power" of the monetary unit—in this case, of the gold ounce. It tells what that ounce can purchase in exchange, just as the money-price of a television set tells how much money a television set can bring in exchange.

What determines the price of money? The same forces that determine all prices on the market—that venerable but eternally true law: "supply and demand." We all know that if the supply of eggs increases, the price will tend to fall; if the buyers' demand for eggs increases, the price will tend to rise. The same is true for money. An increase in the supply of money will tend to lower its "price;" an increase in the demand for money will raise it. But what is the demand for money? In the case of eggs, we know what "demand" means; it is the amount of money consumers are willing to spend on eggs, plus eggs retained and not sold by suppliers. Similarly, in the case of money, "demand" means the various goods offered in exchange for money, plus the money retained in cash and not spent over a certain time period. In both cases, "supply" may refer to the total stock of the good on the market.

What happens, then, if the supply of gold increases, demand for money remaining the same? The "price of money" falls, i.e., the purchasing power of the money-unit will fall all along the line. An ounce of gold will now be worth less than 100 loaves of bread, 1/3 of a television set, etc. Conversely, if the supply of gold falls, the purchasing power of the gold-ounce rises.

What is the effect of a change in the money supply? Following the example of David Hume, one of the first economists, we may ask ourselves what would happen if, overnight, some good fairy slipped into pockets, purses, and bank vaults, and doubled our supply of money. In our example, she magically doubled our supply of gold. Would we be twice as rich? Obviously not. What makes us rich is an abundance of goods, and what limits that abundance is a scarcity of resources: namely land, labor, and capital. Multiplying coin will not whisk these resources into being. We may *feel* twice as rich for the moment, but clearly all we are doing is *diluting* the money supply. As the public rushes out to spend its new-found wealth, prices will, very roughly, double—or at least rise until the demand is satisfied, and money no longer bids against itself for the existing goods.

Thus, we see that while an increase in the money supply, like an increase in the supply of any good, lowers its price, the change *does not—unlike other goods—confer a social benefit*. The public at large is not made richer. Whereas new consumer or capital goods add to standards of living, new money only raises prices—i.e., dilutes its own purchasing power. The reason for this puzzle is that money is *only useful for its exchange value*. Other goods have various "real" utilities, so that an increase in their supply satisfies more consumer wants. Money has only utility for prospective exchange; its utility lies in its exchange value, or "purchasing power." Our law—that an increase in money does not confer a social benefit—stems from its unique use as a medium of exchange.

An increase in the money supply, then, only dilutes the effectiveness of each gold ounce; on the other hand, a fall in the supply of money raises the power of each gold ounce to do its work. We come to the startling truth that it *doesn't matter what the supply of money is*. Any supply will do as well as any other supply. The free market will simply adjust by changing the purchasing power, or effectiveness of the gold-unit. There is no need to tamper with the market in order to alter the money supply that it determines.

At this point, the monetary planner might object: "All right, granting that it is pointless to increase the money supply, isn't gold mining a waste of resources? Shouldn't the government keep the money supply constant, and prohibit new mining?" This argument might be plausible to those who hold no principled objections to government meddling, though it would not convince the determined advocate of liberty. But the objection overlooks an important point: that gold is not only money, but is also, inevitably, a *commodity*. An increased supply of gold may not confer any *monetary* benefit, but it does confer a *nonmonetary* benefit—i.e., it does increase the supply of gold used in consumption (ornaments, dental work, and the like) and in production (industrial work). Gold mining, therefore, is not a social waste at all.

We conclude, therefore, that determining the supply of money, like all other goods, is best left to the free market. Aside from the general moral and economic advantages of freedom over coercion, no dictated quantity of money will do the work better, and the free market will set the production of gold in accordance with its relative ability to satisfy the needs of consumers, as compared with all other productive goods.[10]

9.
The Problem of "Hoarding"

The critic of monetary freedom is not so easily silenced, however. There is, in particular, the ancient bugbear of "hoarding." The image is conjured up of the selfish old

---

[10]Gold mining is, of course, no more profitable than any other business; in the long-run, its rate of return will be equal to the net rate of return in any other industry.

miser who, perhaps irrationally, perhaps from evil motives, hoards up gold unused in his cellar or treasure trove— thereby stopping the flow of circulation and trade, causing depressions and other problems. Is hoarding really a menace?

In the first place, what has simply happened is an increased demand for money on the part of the miser. As a result, prices of goods fall, and the purchasing power of the gold-ounce rises. There has been no loss to society, which simply carries on with a lower active supply of more "powerful" gold ounces.

Even in the worst possible view of the matter, then, nothing has gone wrong, and monetary freedom creates no difficulties. But there is more to the problem than that. For it is by no means irrational for people to desire *more* or *less* money in their cash balances.

Let us, at this point, study cash balances further. Why do people keep any cash balances at all? Suppose that all of us were able to foretell the future with absolute certainty. In that case, no one would have to keep cash balances on hand. Everyone would know exactly how much he will spend, and how much income he will receive, at all future dates. He need not keep any money at hand, but will lend out his gold so as to receive his payments in the needed amounts on the very days he makes his expenditures. But, of course, we necessarily live in a world of *uncertainty*. People do not precisely know what will happen to them, or what their future incomes or costs will be. The more uncertain and fearful they are, the more cash balances they will want to hold; the more secure, the less cash they will wish to keep on hand. Another reason for keeping cash is also a function of the real world of uncertainty. If people expect the price of money to fall in the near future, they will spend their money now while money is more valuable, thus "dishoarding" and reducing their demand for money. Conversely, if they expect the price of money to rise, they will wait to spend money later when it is more valuable, and their demand for cash will increase. People's demands for cash balances, then, rise and fall for good and sound reasons.

Economists err if they believe something is wrong when money is not in constant, active "circulation." Money is only useful for exchange value, true, *but it is not only useful at the actual moment of exchange*. This truth has been often overlooked. Money is just as useful when lying "idle" in somebody's cash balance, even in a miser's "hoard."[11] For that money is being held now in wait for possible future exchange—it supplies to its owner, right now, the usefulness of permitting exchanges at any time—present or future—the owner might desire.

It should be remembered that all gold must be owned by someone, and therefore that all gold must be held in people's cash balances. If there are 3,000 tons of gold in the society, all 3,000 tons must be owned and held, at any one time, in the cash balances of individual people. The total sum of cash balances is always identical with the total supply of money in the society. Thus, ironically, if it were not for the uncertainty of the real world, there could be no monetary system at all! In a certain world, no one would be willing to hold cash, so the demand for money in society would fall infinitely, prices would skyrocket without end, and any

---

[11]At what point does a man's cash balance become a faintly disreputable "hoard," or the prudent man a miser? It is impossible to fix any definite criterion: generally, the charge of "hoarding" means that *A* is keeping more cash than *B* thinks is appropriate for *A*.

monetary system would break down. Instead of the existence of cash balances being an annoying and troublesome factor, interfering with monetary exchange, it is absolutely necessary to any monetary economy.

It is misleading, furthermore, to say that money "circulates." Like all metaphors taken from the physical sciences, it connotes some sort of mechanical process, independent of human will, which moves at a certain speed of flow, or "velocity." Actually, money does not "circulate"; it is, from time, to time, *transferred* from one person's cash balance to another's. The existence of money, once again, depends upon people's willingness to hold cash balances.

At the beginning of this section, we saw that "hoarding" never brings any loss to society. Now, we will see that movement in the price of money caused by changes in the demand for money yields a positive social benefit—as positive as any conferred by increased supplies of goods and services. We have seen that the total sum of cash balances in society is equal and identical with the total supply of money. Let us assume the supply remains constant, say at 3,000 tons. Now, suppose, for whatever reason—perhaps growing apprehension—people's demand for cash balances increases. Surely, it is a positive social benefit to satisfy this demand. But how can it be satisfied when the total sum of cash must remain the same? Simply as follows: with people valuing cash balances more highly, the demand for money increases, and prices fall. As a result, the same total sum of cash balances now confers a higher "real" balance, i.e., it is higher in proportion to the prices of goods—to the work that money has to perform. In short, the effective cash balances of the public have increased. Conversely, a fall in the demand for cash will cause increased spending and higher prices. The public's desire for lower effective cash balances will be satisfied by the necessity for given total cash to perform more work.

Therefore, while a change in the price of money stemming from changes in supply merely alters the effectiveness of the money-unit and confers no social benefit, a fall or rise caused by a change in the *demand for* cash balances *does* yield a social benefit—for it satisfies a public desire for either a higher or lower proportion of cash balances to the work done by cash. On the other hand, an increased *supply* of money will *frustrate* public demand for a more *effective* sum total of cash (more effective in terms of purchasing power).

People will almost always say, if asked, that they want as much money as they can get! But what they really want is not more units of money—more gold ounces or "dollars"— but more *effective* units, i.e., greater command of goods and services bought by money. We have seen that society cannot satisfy its demand for more money by increasing its supply—for an increased supply will simply *dilute* the effectiveness of each ounce, and the money will be no more really plentiful than before. People's standard of living (except in the nonmonetary uses of gold) cannot increase by mining more gold. If people want more effective gold ounces in their cash balances, they can get them only through a fall in prices and a rise in the effectiveness of each ounce.

10.
Stabilize the Price Level?

Some theorists charge that a free monetary system would be unwise, because it would not "stabilize the price level," i.e., the price of the money-unit. Money, they say, is supposed to be a fixed yardstick that never changes. Therefore, its value, or purchasing power, should be stabilized. Since the price of money would admittedly fluctuate on the free market, freedom must be overruled by government management to insure stability.[12] Stability would provide justice, for example, to debtors and creditors, who will be sure of paying back dollars, or gold ounces, of the same purchasing power as they lent out.

Yet, if creditors and debtors want to hedge against future changes in purchasing power, they can do so easily on the free market. When they make their contracts, they can agree that repayment will be made in a sum of money *adjusted* by some agreed-upon index number of changes in the value of money. The stabilizers have long advocated such measures, but strangely enough, the very lenders and borrowers who are supposed to benefit most from stability, have rarely availed themselves of the opportunity. Must the government then *force* certain "benefits" on people who have already freely rejected them? Apparently, businessmen would rather take their chances, in this world of irremediable uncertainty, on their ability to anticipate the conditions of the market. After all, the price of money is no different from any other free price on the market. They can change in response to changes in demand of individuals; why not the monetary price?

Artificial stabilization would, in fact, seriously distort and hamper the workings of the market. As we have indicated, people would be unavoidably frustrated in their desires to alter their real proportion of cash balances; there

---

[12]How the government would go about this is unimportant at this point. Basically, it would involve governmentally-managed changes in the money supply.

would be no opportunity to change cash balances in proportion to prices. Furthermore, improved standards of living come to the public from the fruits of capital investment. Increased productivity tends to lower prices (and costs) and thereby distribute the fruits of free enterprise to all the public, raising the standard of living of all consumers. Forcible propping up of the price level prevents this spread of higher living standards.

Money, in short, is not a "fixed yardstick." It is a commodity serving as a medium for exchanges. Flexibility in its value in response to consumer demands is just as important and just as beneficial as any other free pricing on the market.

11.
Coexisting Moneys

So far we have obtained the following picture of money in a purely free economy: gold or silver coming to be used as a medium of exchange; gold minted by competitive private firms, circulating by weight; prices fluctuating freely on the market in response to consumer demands and supplies of productive resources. Freedom of prices necessarily implies freedom of movement for the purchasing power of the money-unit; it would be impossible to use force and interfere with movements in the value of money without simultaneously crippling freedom of prices for all goods. The resulting free economy would *not* be chaotic. On the contrary, the economy would move swiftly and efficiently to supply the wants of consumers. The money market can also be free.

Thus far, we have simplified the problem by assuming only one monetary metal—say, gold. Suppose that *two* or

more moneys continue to circulate on the world market—
say, gold and silver. Possibly, gold will be the money in one
area and silver in another, or else they both may circulate
side by side. Gold, for example, being ounce-for-ounce
more valuable on the market than silver, may be used for
larger transactions and silver for smaller. Would not two
moneys be impossibly chaotic? Wouldn't the government
have to step in and impose a fixed ration between the two
("bimetallism") or in some way demonetize one or the
other metal (impose a "single standard")?

It is very possible that the market, given free rein, might
eventually establish one single metal as money. But in
recent centuries, silver stubbornly remained to challenge
gold. It is not necessary, however, for the government to step
in and save the market from its own folly in maintaining
two moneys. Silver remained in circulation precisely
because it was convenient (for small change, for example).
Silver and gold could easily circulate side by side, and have
done so in the past. The relative supplies of and demands
for the two metals will determine the exchange rate between
the two, and this rate, *like any other price*, will continually
fluctuate in response to these changing forces. At one time,
for example, silver and gold ounces might exchange at 16:1,
another time at 15:1, etc. Which metal will serve as a unit
of account depends on the concrete circumstances of the
market. If gold is the money of account, then most transactions will be reckoned in gold ounces, and silver ounces will
exchange at a freely-fluctuating price in terms of the gold.

It should be clear that the exchange rate and the purchasing powers of the units of the two metals will always
tend to be proportional. If prices of goods are fifteen times
as much in silver as they are in gold, then the exchange rate
will tend to be set at 15:1. If not, it will pay to exchange from

one to the other until parity is reached. Thus, if prices are fifteen times as much in terms of silver as gold while silver/gold is 20:1, people will rush to sell their goods for gold, buy silver, and then rebuy the goods with silver, reaping a handsome gain in the process. This will quickly restore the "purchasing power parity" of the exchange rate; as gold gets cheaper in terms of silver, silver prices of goods go up, and gold prices of goods go down.

The free market, in short, is eminently *orderly* not only when money is free but even when there is more than one money circulating.

What kind of "standard" will a free money provide? The important thing is that the standard not be imposed by government decree. If left to itself, the market may establish gold as a single money ("gold standard"), silver as a single money ("silver standard"), or, perhaps most likely, both as moneys with freely-fluctuating exchange rates ("parallel standards").[13]

---

[13]For historical examples of parallel standards, see W. Stanley Jevons, *Money and the Mechanism of Exchange* (London: Kegan Paul, 1905), pp. 88–96, and Robert S. Lopez, "Back to Gold, 1252," *Economic History Review* (December 1956): 224. Gold coinage was introduced into modern Europe almost simultaneously in Genoa and Florence. Florence instituted bimetallism, while "Genoa, on the contrary, in conformity to the principle of restricting state intervention as much as possible, did not try to enforce a fixed relation between coins of different metals," ibid. On the theory of parallel standards, see Mises, *Theory of Money and Credit*, pp. 179f. For a proposal that the United States go onto a parallel standard, by an official of the U.S. Assay Office, see I.W. Sylvester, *Bullion Certificates as Currency* (New York, 1882).

12.
Money Warehouses

Suppose, then, that the free market has established gold as money (forgetting again about silver for the sake of simplicity). Even in the convenient shape of coins, gold is often cumbersome and awkward to carry and use directly in exchange. For larger transactions, it is awkward and expensive to transport several hundred pounds of gold. But the free market, ever ready to satisfy social needs, comes to the rescue. Gold, in the first place, must be stored somewhere, and just as specialization is most efficient in other lines of business, so it will be most efficient in the warehousing business. Certain firms, then, will be successful on the market in providing warehousing services. Some will be gold warehouses, and will store gold for its myriad owners. As in the case of all warehouses, the owner's right to the stored goods is established by a *warehouse receipt* which he receives in exchange for storing the goods. The receipt entitles the owner to claim his goods at any time he desires. This warehouse will earn profit no differently from any other—i.e., by charging a price for its storage services.

There is every reason to believe that gold warehouses, or money warehouses, will flourish on the free market in the same way that other warehouses will prosper. In fact, warehousing plays an even more important role in the case of money. For all other goods pass into consumption, and so must leave the warehouse after a while to be used up in production or consumption. But money, as we have seen, is mainly not "used" in the physical sense; instead, it is used to exchange for other goods, and to lie in wait for such exchanges in the future. In short, money is not so much "used up" as simply transferred from one person to another.

In such a situation, convenience inevitably leads to *transfer of the warehouse receipt instead of the physical gold itself*. Suppose, for example, that Smith and Jones both store their gold in the same warehouse. Jones sells Smith an automobile for 100 gold ounces. They could go through the expensive process of Smith's redeeming his receipt, and moving their gold to Jones's office, with Jones turning right around and redepositing the gold again. But they will undoubtedly choose a far more convenient course: Smith simply gives Jones a warehouse receipt for 100 ounces of gold.

In this way, warehouse receipts for money come more and more to function as *money substitutes*. Fewer and fewer transactions move the actual gold; in more and more cases paper titles to the gold are used instead. As the market develops, there will be three limits on the advance of this substitution process. *One* is the extent that people us these money warehouses—called *banks*—instead of cash. Clearly, if Jones, for some reason, didn't like to use a bank, Smith would have to transport the actual gold. The *second* limit is the extent of the clientele of *each bank*. In other words, the more transactions taking place between clients of *different* banks, the more gold will have to be transported. The more exchanges are made by clients of the same bank, the less need to transport the gold. If Jones and Smith were clients of different warehouses, Smith's bank (or Smith himself) would have to transport the gold to Jones's bank. *Third*, the clientele must have confidence in the trustworthiness of their banks. If they suddenly find out, for example, that the bank officials have had criminal records, the bank will likely lose its business in short order. In this respect, all warehouses—and all businesses resting on good will—are alike.

As banks grow and confidence in them develops, their clients may find it more convenient in many cases to waive their right to paper receipts—called *bank notes*—and, *instead, to keep their titles as open book accounts*. In the monetary realm, these have been called *bank deposits*. Instead of transferring paper receipts, the client has a book claim at the bank; he makes exchanges by writing an order to his warehouse to transfer a portion of this account to someone else. Thus, in our example, Smith will order the bank to transfer book title to his 100 gold ounces to Jones. This written order is called a *check*.

It should be clear that, economically, there is no difference whatever between a bank note and a bank deposit. Both are claims to ownership of stored gold; both are transferred similarly as money substitutes, and both have the identical three limits on their extent of use. The client can choose, according to this convenience, whether he wishes to keep his title in note, or deposit, form.[14]

Now, what has happened to their money supply as a result of all these operations? If paper notes or bank deposits are used as "money substitutes," does this mean that the effective money supply in the economy has increased even though the stock of gold has remained the same? Certainly not. For the money substitutes are simply warehouse receipts for actually-deposited gold. If Jones deposits 100 ounces of gold in his warehouse and gets a receipt for it, the receipt can be used on the market as money, but only as a convenient *stand-in* for the gold, not as an increment. The gold in the vault is then no longer a part

---

[14]A third form of money-substitute will be *token coins* for very small change. These are, in effect, equivalent to bank notes, but "printed" on base metal rather than on paper.

of the effective money supply, but is held as a *reserve* for its receipt, to be claimed whenever desired by its owner. An increase or decrease in the use of substitutes, then, exerts no change on the money supply. Only the *form* of the supply is changed, not the total. Thus the money supply of a community may begin as ten million gold ounces. Then, six million may be deposited in banks, in return for gold notes, whereupon the effective supply will now be: four million ounces of gold, six million ounces of gold claims in paper notes. The total money supply has remained the same.

Curiously, many people have argued that it would be impossible for banks to make money if they were to operate on this "100 percent reserve" basis (gold always represented by its receipt). Yet, there is no real problem, any more than for any warehouse. Almost all warehouses keep all the goods for their owners (100 percent reserve) as a matter of course—in fact, it would be considered fraud or theft to do otherwise. Their profits are earned from service charges to their customers. The banks can charge for their services in the same way. If it is objected that customers will not pay the high service charges, this means that the banks' services are not in very great demand, and the use of their services will fall to the levels that consumers find worthwhile.

We come now to perhaps the thorniest problem facing the monetary economist: an evaluation of "fractional reserve banking." We must ask the question: would fractional reserve banking be permitted in a free market, or would it be proscribed as fraud? It is well-known that banks have rarely stayed on a "100 percent" basis very long. Since money can remain in the warehouse for a long period of time, the bank is tempted to use some of the money for its own account—tempted also because people do not ordinarily care whether the gold coins they receive back from the warehouse are the identical gold coins they deposited. The bank is tempted, then to use other people's money to earn a profit for itself.

If the banks lend out the gold directly, the receipts, of course, are now partially invalidated. There are now some receipts with no gold behind them; in short, the bank is effectively insolvent, since it cannot possibly meet its own obligations if called upon to do so. It cannot possibly hand over its customers' property, should they all so desire.

Generally, banks, instead of taking the gold directly, print uncovered or "pseudo" warehouse receipts, i.e., warehouse receipts for gold that is not and cannot be there. These are then loaned at a profit. Clearly, the economic effect is the same. More warehouse receipts are printed than gold exists in the vaults. What the bank has done is to issue gold warehouse receipts which represent nothing, but are supposed to represent 100 percent of their face value in gold. The pseudo-receipts pour forth on the trusting market in the same way as the true receipts, and thus add to the effective money supply of the country. In the above example, if the banks now issue two million ounces of false receipts, with no gold behind them, the money supply of the country will rise from ten to twelve million gold ounces—at least until the hocus-pocus has been discovered and corrected. There are now, in addition to four million ounces of gold held by the public, eight million ounces of money substitutes, only six million of which are covered by gold.

Issue of pseudo-receipts, like counterfeiting of coin, is an example of *inflation*, which will be studied further below. *Inflation* may be defined as *any increase in the economy's supply of money not consisting of an increase in the stock of the money metal*. Fractional reserve banks, therefore, are inherently inflationary institutions.

Defenders of banks reply as follows: the banks are simply functioning like other businesses—they take risks. Admittedly, if all the depositors presented their claims, the banks would be bankrupt, since outstanding receipts exceed gold in the vaults. But, banks simply take the chance—usually justified—that not everyone will ask for his gold. The great difference, however, between the "fractional reserve" bank and all other business is this: other businessmen use their own or borrowed capital in ventures, and if they borrow credit, they promise to pay at a future date, taking care to have enough money at hand on that date to meet their obligation. If Smith borrows 100 gold ounces for a year, he will arrange to have 100 gold ounces available on that future date. But the bank isn't borrowing from its depositors; it doesn't pledge to pay back gold at a certain date in the future. Instead, it pledges to pay the receipt in gold at any time, on demand. In short, the bank note or deposit is not an IOU, or debt; it is a warehouse receipt for other people's property. Further, when a businessman borrows or lends money, he does not add to the money supply. The loaned funds are *saved* funds, part of the existing money supply being transferred from saver to borrower. Bank issues, on the other hand, artificially increase the money supply since pseudo-receipts are injected into the market.

A bank, then, is not taking the usual business risk. It does not, like all businessmen, arrange the time pattern of its assets proportionately to the time pattern of liabilities, i.e., see to it that it will have enough money, on due dates, to pay its bills. Instead, most of its liabilities are instantaneous, but its assets are not.

The bank creates new money out of thin air, and does not, like everyone else, have to acquire money by producing and selling its services. In short, the bank is *already* and at all times bankrupt; but its bankruptcy is only *revealed* when customers get suspicious and precipitate "bank runs." No other business experiences a phenomenon like a "run." No other business can be plunged into bankruptcy overnight simply because its customers decide to repossess their own property. No other business creates fictitious new money, which will evaporate when truly gauged.

The dire economic effects of fractional bank money will be explored in the next chapter. Here we conclude that, morally, such banking would have no more right to exist in a truly free market than any other form of implicit theft. It is true that the note or deposit does not actually say on its face that the warehouse guarantees to keep a full backing of gold on hand at all times. But the bank does promise to redeem on demand, and so when it issues any fake receipts, it is already committing fraud, since it immediately becomes impossible for the bank to keep its pledge and redeem all of its notes and deposits.[15] Fraud, therefore, is immediately being committed when the act of issuing pseudo-receipts takes place. *Which* particular receipts are fraudulent can only be discovered *after* a run on the bank has occurred (since all the receipts look alike), and the late-coming claimants are left high and dry.[16]

---

[15]See Amasa Walker, *The Science of Wealth*, 3rd ed. (Boston: Little, Brown, 1867), pp. 139–41; and pp. 126–232 for an excellent discussion of the problems of a fractional-reserve money.

[16]Perhaps a libertarian system would consider "general warrant deposits" (which allow the warehouse to return any homogeneous good to the

If fraud is to be proscribed in a free society, then fractional reserve banking would have to meet the same fate.[17] Suppose, however, that fraud and fractional reserve banking are permitted, with the banks only required to fulfill their obligations to redeem in gold on demand. Any failure to do so would mean instant bankruptcy. Such a system has come to be known as "free banking." Would there then be a heavy fraudulent issue of money substitutes, with resulting artificial creation of new money? Many people have assumed so, and believed that "wildcat banking" would then simply inflate the money supply astronomically. But, on the contrary, "free banking" would lead to a far "harder" monetary system than we have today.

The banks would be checked by the same three limits that we noted above, and checked rather rigorously. In the first place, each bank's expansion will be limited by a loss of gold to another bank. For a bank can only expand money within the limits of its *own* clientele. Suppose, for example, that Bank *A*, with 10,000 ounces of gold deposited, now issues 2,000 ounces of false warehouse receipts to gold, and lends them to various enterprises, or invests them in securities. The borrower, or former holder of securities, will spend

---

depositor) as "specific warrant deposits," which, like bills of lading, pawn tickets, dock warrants, etc., establish ownership to certain specific earmarked objects. For, in the case of a general deposit warrant, the warehouse is tempted to treat the goods as its *own* property, instead of being the property of its customers. This is precisely what the banks have been doing. See Jevons, *Money and the Medium of Exchange*, pp. 207–12.

[17]Fraud is *implicit* theft, since it means that a contract has not been completed after the value has been received. In short, if *A* sells *B* a box labeled "corn flakes" and it turns out to be straw upon opening, *A*'s fraud is really theft of *B*'s property. Similarly, the issue of warehouse receipts for nonexistent goods, identical with genuine receipts, is fraud upon those who possess claims to nonexistent property.

the new money on various goods and services. Eventually, the money going the rounds will reach an owner who is a client of *another* bank, *B*.

At that point, Bank *B* will call upon Bank *A* to redeem its receipt in gold, so that the gold can be transferred to Bank *B*'s vaults. Clearly, the wider the extent of each bank's clientele, and the more the clients trade with one another, the more scope there is for each bank to expand its credit and money supply. For if the bank's clientele is narrow, then soon after its issue of created money, it will be called upon to redeem—and, as we have seen, it doesn't have the wherewithal to redeem more than a fraction of its obligations. To avoid the threat of bankruptcy from this quarter, then, the narrower the scope of a bank's clientele, the greater the fraction of gold it must keep in reserve, and the less it can expand. If there is one bank in each country, there will be far more scope for expansion than if there is one bank for every two persons in the community. Other things being equal, then, the more banks there are, and the tinier their size, the "harder"—and better—the monetary supply will be. Similarly, a bank's clientele will also be limited by those who don't use a bank at all. The more people use actual gold instead of bank money, the less room there is for bank inflation.

Suppose, however, that the banks form a cartel, and agree to pay out each other's receipts, and not call for redemption. And suppose further that bank money is in universal use. Are there any limits left on bank expansion? Yes, there remains the check of client confidence in the banks. As bank credit and the money supply expand further and further, more and more clients will get worried over the lowering of the reserve fraction. And, in a truly free society, those who know the truth about the real insolvency of the

banking system will be able to form AntiBank Leagues to
urge clients to get their money out before it is too late. In
short, leagues to urge bank runs, or the threat of their for-
mation, will be able to stop and reverse the monetary
expansion.

None of this discussion is meant to impugn the general
practice of *credit*, which has an important and vital function
on the free market. In a credit transaction, the possessor of
money (a good useful in the present) exchanges it for an
IOU payable at some future date (the IOU being a "future
good") and the interest charge reflects the higher valuation
of present goods over future goods on the market. But bank
notes or deposits are *not* credit; they are warehouse receipts,
instantaneous claims to cash (e.g., gold) in the bank vaults.
The debtor makes sure that he pays his debt when payment
becomes due; the fractional reserve banker can never pay
more than a small fraction of his outstanding liabilities.

We turn, in the next chapter, to a study of the various
forms of governmental interference in the monetary system—most of them designed, not to repress fraudulent
issue, but on the contrary, to remove these and other natural checks on inflation.

13.
Summary

What have we learned about money in a free society?
We have learned that *all* money has originated, and must
originate, in a useful commodity chosen by the free market
as a medium of exchange. The unit of money is simply a
unit of weight of the monetary commodity—usually a
metal, such as gold or silver. Under freedom, the commodities chosen as money, their shape and form, are left to the

voluntary decisions of free individuals. Private coinage, therefore, is just as legitimate and worthwhile as any business activity. The "price" of money is its purchasing power in terms of all goods in the economy, and this is determined by its supply, and by every individual's demand for money. Any attempt by government to fix the price will interfere with the satisfaction of people's demands for money. If people find it more convenient to use more than one metal as money, the exchange rate between them on the market will be determined by the relative demands and supplies, and will tend to equal the ratios of their respective purchasing power. Once there is enough supply of a metal to permit the market to choose it as money, no increase in supply can improve its monetary function. An increase in money supply will then merely dilute the effectiveness of each ounce of money without helping the economy. An increased stock of gold or silver, however, fulfills more *non*monetary wants (ornament, industrial purposes, etc.) served by the metal, and is therefore socially useful. Inflation (an increase in money substitutes not covered by an increase in the metal stock) is never socially useful, but merely benefits one set of people at the expense of another. Inflation, being a fraudulent invasion of property, could not take place on the free market.

In sum, freedom can run a monetary system as superbly as it runs the rest of the economy. Contrary to many writers, there is nothing special about money that requires extensive governmental dictation. Here, too, free men will best and most smoothly supply all their economic wants. For money as for all other activities of man, "liberty is the mother, not the daughter, of order."

III.
GOVERNMENT MEDDLING
WITH MONEY

1.
The Revenue of Government

GOVERNMENTS, IN CONTRAST TO all other organizations, do not obtain their revenue as payment for their services. Consequently, governments face an economic problem different from that of everyone else. Private individuals who want to acquire more goods and services from others must produce and sell more of what others want. Governments need only find some method of expropriating more goods without the owner's consent.

In a barter economy, government officials can only expropriate resources in one way: by seizing goods *in kind*. In a monetary economy they will find it easier to seize *monetary* assets, and then use the money to acquire goods and services for government, or else pay the money as subsidies to favored groups. Such seizure is called *taxation*.[1]

---

[1]Direct seizure of goods is therefore not now as extensive as monetary expropriation. Instances of the former still occurring are "due process" seizure of land under eminent domain, quartering of troops in an occupied country, and especially compulsory confiscation of labor service (e.g., military conscription, compulsory jury duty, and forcing business to keep tax records and collect withholding taxes).

Taxation, however, is often unpopular, and, in less temperate days, frequently precipitated revolutions. The emergence of money, while a boon to the human race, also opened a more subtle route for governmental expropriation of resources. On the free market, money can be acquired by producing and selling goods and services that people want, or by mining (a business no more profitable, in the long run, than any other). But if government can find ways to engage in *counterfeiting*—the creation of new money out of thin air—it can quickly produce its own money without taking the trouble to sell services or mine gold. It can then appropriate resources slyly and almost unnoticed, without rousing the hostility touched off by taxation. In fact, counterfeiting can create in its very victims the blissful illusion of unparalleled prosperity.

Counterfeiting is evidently but another name for inflation—both creating new "money" that is not standard gold or silver, and both functioning similarly. And now we see why governments are inherently inflationary: because inflation is a powerful and subtle means for government acquisition of the public's resources, a painless and all the more dangerous form of taxation.

2.
The Economic Effects of Inflation

To gauge the economic effects of inflation, let us see what happens when a group of counterfeiters set about their work. Suppose the economy has a supply of 10,000 gold ounces, and counterfeiters, so cunning that they cannot be detected, pump in 2,000 "ounces" more. What will be the consequences? First, there will be a clear gain to the counterfeiters. They take the newly-created money and use it to buy goods and services. In the words of the famous *New Yorker* cartoon, showing a group of counterfeiters in sober contemplation of their handiwork: "Retail spending is about to get a needed shot in the arm." Precisely. Local spending, indeed, *does* get a shot in the arm. The new money works its way, step by step, throughout the economic system. As the new money spreads, it bids prices up—as we have seen, new money can only dilute the effectiveness of each dollar. But this dilution takes time and is therefore uneven; in the meantime, some people gain and other people lose. In short, the counterfeiters and their local retailers have found their incomes increased before any rise in the prices of the things they buy. But, on the other hand, people in remote areas of the economy, who have not yet received the new money, find their buying prices rising before their incomes. Retailers at the other end of the country, for example, will suffer losses. The first receivers of the new money gain most, and at the expense of the latest receivers.

Inflation, then, confers no general social benefit; instead, it redistributes the wealth in favor of the first-comers and at the expense of the laggards in the race. And inflation is, in effect, a race—to see who can get the new money earliest. The latecomers—the ones stuck with the loss—are often called the "fixed income groups." Ministers, teachers, people on salaries, lag notoriously behind other groups in acquiring the new money. Particular sufferers will be those depending on fixed money contracts— contracts made in the days before the inflationary rise in prices. Life insurance beneficiaries and annuitants, retired persons living off pensions, landlords with long term leases, bondholders and other creditors, those holding cash, all will bear the brunt of the inflation. They will be the ones who are "taxed."[2]

Inflation has other disastrous effects. It distorts that keystone of our economy: business calculation. Since prices do not all change uniformly and at the same speed, it becomes very difficult for business to separate the lasting from the transitional, and gauge truly the demands of consumers or the cost of their operations. For example, accounting practice enters the "cost" of an asset at the amount the business has paid for it. But if inflation intervenes, the cost of replacing the asset when it wears out will be far greater than that recorded on the books. As a result, business accounting will seriously overstate their profits during inflation—and may even consume capital while presumably increasing their investments.[3] Similarly, stockholders and real estate holders will acquire capital gains during an inflation that are not really "gains" at all. But they may spend part of these gains without realizing that they are thereby consuming their original capital.

By creating illusory profits and distorting economic calculation, inflation will suspend the free market's penalizing of inefficient, and rewarding of efficient, firms. Almost all

---

[2]It has become fashionable to scoff at the concern displayed by "conservatives" for the "widows and orphans" hurt by inflation. And yet this is precisely one of the chief problems that must be faced. Is it really "progressive" to rob widows and orphans and to use the proceeds to subsidize farmers and armament workers?

[3]This error will be greatest in those firms with the oldest equipment, and in the most heavily capitalized industries. An undue number of firms, therefore, will pour into these industries during an inflation. For further discussion of this accounting-cost error, see W.T. Baxter, "The Accountant's Contribution to the Trade Cycle," *Economica* (May 1955): 99–112.

firms will seemingly prosper. The general atmosphere of a "sellers' market" will lead to a decline in the quality of goods and of service to consumers, since consumers often resist price increases less when they occur in the form of downgrading of quality.[4] The quality of work will decline in an inflation for a more subtle reason: people become enamored of "get-rich-quick" schemes, seemingly within their grasp in an era of ever-rising prices, and often scorn sober effort. Inflation also penalizes thrift and encourages debt, for any sum of money loaned will be repaid in dollars of lower purchasing power than when originally received. The incentive, then, is to borrow and repay later rather than save and lend. Inflation, therefore, lowers the general standard of living in the very course of creating a tinsel atmosphere of "prosperity."

Fortunately, inflation cannot go on forever. For eventually people wake up to this form of taxation; they wake up to the continual shrinkage in the purchasing power of their dollar.

At first, when prices rise, people say: "Well, this is abnormal, the product of some emergency. I will postpone my purchases and wait until prices go back down." This is the common attitude during the first phase of an inflation. This notion moderates the price rise itself, and conceals the inflation further, since the demand for money is thereby increased. But, as inflation proceeds, people begin to realize that prices are going up perpetually as a result of perpetual inflation. Now people will say: "I will buy now, though prices are 'high,' because if I wait, prices will go up

---

[4]In these days of rapt attention to "cost-of-living indexes" (e.g., escalator-wage contracts) there is strong incentive to increase prices in such a way that the change will not be revealed in the index.

still further." As a result, the demand for money now falls
and prices go up *more*, proportionately, than the increase in
the money supply. At this point, the government is often
called upon to "relieve the money shortage" caused by the
accelerated price rise, and it inflates even faster. Soon, the
country reaches the stage of the "crack-up boom," when
people say: "I must buy anything now—anything to get rid
of money which depreciates on my hands." The supply of
money skyrockets, the demand plummets, and prices rise
astronomically. Production falls sharply, as people spend
more and more of their time finding ways to get rid of their
money. The monetary system has, in effect, broken down
completely, and the economy reverts to other moneys, if
they are attainable—other metal, foreign currencies if this is
a one-country inflation, or even a return to barter conditions. The monetary system has broken down under the
impact of inflation.

This condition of *hyper-inflation* is familiar historically
in the *assignats* of the French Revolution, the Continentals
of the American Revolution, and especially the German crisis of 1923, and the Chinese and other currencies after
World War II.[5]

A final indictment of inflation is that whenever the
newly issued money is first used as loans to business, inflation causes the dread "business cycle." This silent but
deadly process, undetected for generations, works as follows: new money is issued by the banking system, under the
aegis of government, and loaned to business. To businessmen, the new funds seem to be genuine investments, but
these funds do not, like free-market investments, arise from

---

[5]On the German example, see Costantino Bresciani-Turroni, *The Economics of Inflation* (London: George Allen and Unwin, 1937).

voluntary savings. The new money is invested by businessmen in various projects, and paid out to workers and other
factors as higher wages and prices. As the new money filters
down to the whole economy, the people tend to re-establish
their old voluntary consumption/saving proportions. In
short, if people wish to save and invest about 20 percent of
their incomes and consume the rest, new bank money
loaned to business at first makes the saving proportion look
higher. When the new money seeps down to the public, it
re-establishes its old 20–80 proportion, and many investments are now revealed to be wasteful. Liquidation of the
wasteful investments of the inflationary boom constitutes
the *depression* phase of the business cycle.[6]

3.
Compulsory Monopoly of the Mint

For government to use counterfeiting to add to its revenue, many lengthy steps must be travelled down the road
away from the free market. Government could not simply
invade a functioning free market and print its own paper
tickets. Done so abruptly, few people would accept the government's money. Even in modern times, many people in
"backward countries" have simply refused to accept paper
money, and insist on trading only in gold. Governmental
incursion, therefore, must be far more subtle and gradual.

---

[6]For a further discussion, see Murray N. Rothbard, *America's Great Depression* (Princeton, N.J.: D. Van Nostrand, 1963), Part I.

Until a few centuries ago, there were no banks, and therefore the government could not use the banking engine for massive inflation as it can today. What could it do when only gold and silver circulated?

The first step, taken firmly by every sizeable government, was to seize an absolute monopoly of the *minting* business. That was the indispensable means of getting control of the coinage supply. The king's or the lord's picture was stamped upon coins, and the myth was propagated that coinage is an essential prerogative of royal or baronial "sovereignty." The mintage monopoly allowed government to supply whatever denominations of coin it, and not the public, wanted. As a result, the variety of coins on the market was forcibly reduced. Furthermore, the mint could now charge a high price, greater than costs ("seigniorage"), a price just covering costs ("brassage"), or supply coins free of charge. Seigniorage was a monopoly price, and it imposed a special burden on the conversion of bullion to coin; gratuitous coinage, on the other hand, overstimulated the manufacture of coins from bullion, and forced the general taxpayer to pay for minting services utilized by others.

Having acquired the mintage monopoly, governments fostered the use of the *name* of the monetary unit, doing their best to separate the name from its true base in the underlying weight of the coin. This, too, was a highly important step, for it liberated each government from the necessity of abiding by the common money of the world market. Instead of using grains or grams of gold or silver, each State fostered its own national name in the supposed interests of monetary patriotism: dollars, marks, francs, and the like. The shift made possible the preeminent means of governmental counterfeiting of coin: debasement.

4.

Debasement

Debasement was the State's method of counterfeiting the very coins it had banned private firms from making in the name of vigorous protection of the monetary standard. Sometimes, the government committed simple fraud, secretly diluting gold with a base alloy, making shortweight coins. More characteristically, the mint melted and recoined all the coins of the realm, giving the subjects back the same number of "pounds" or "marks," but of a lighter weight. The leftover ounces of gold or silver were pocketed by the King and used to pay his expenses. In that way, government continually juggled and redefined the very standard it was pledged to protect. The profits of debasement were haughtily claimed as "seigniorage" by the rulers.

Rapid and severe debasement was a hallmark of the Middle Ages, in almost every country in Europe. Thus, in 1200 A.D., the French *livre tournois* was defined at ninety-eight grams of fine silver; by 1600 A.D. it signified only eleven grams. A striking case is the *dinar*, a coin of the Saracens in Spain. The *dinar* originally consisted of sixty-five gold grains, when first coined at the end of the seventh century. The Saracens were notably sound in monetary matters, and by the middle of the twelfth century, the *dinar* was still sixty grains. At that point, the Christian kings conquered Spain, and by the early thirteenth century, the *dinar* (now called *maravedi*) was reduced to fourteen grains. Soon the gold coin was too light to circulate, and it was converted into a *silver* coin weighing twenty-six grains of silver. This, too, was debased, and by the mid-fifteenth century, the *maravedi* was only 1.5 silver grains, and again too small to circulate.[7]

5.
Gresham's Law and Coinage

A. Bimetallism

Government imposes price controls largely in order to divert public attention from governmental inflation to the alleged evils of the free market. As we have seen, "Gresham's Law"—that an artificially overvalued money tends to drive an artificially undervalued money out of circulation—is an example of the general consequences of price control. Government places, in effect, a maximum price on one type of money in terms of the other. Maximum price causes a shortage—disappearance into hoards or exports—of the currency suffering the maximum price (artificially undervalued), and leads it to be replaced in circulation by the overpriced money.

We have seen how this works in the case of new versus worn coins, one of the earliest examples of Gresham's Law. Changing the meaning of money from weight to mere tale, and standardizing denominations for their own rather than for the public's convenience, the governments called new and worn coins by the same name, even though they were of different weight. As a result, people hoarded or exported the full weight new coins, and passed the worn

---

[7]On debasement, see Elgin Groseclose, *Money and Man* (New York: Frederick Ungar, 1961), pp. 57–76.

coins in circulation, with governments hurling maledictions at "speculators," foreigners, or the free market in general, for a condition brought about by the government itself.

A particularly important case of Gresham's Law was the perennial problem of the "standard." We saw that the free market established "parallel standards" of gold and silver, each freely fluctuating in relation to the other in accordance with market supplies and demands. But governments decided they would help out the market by stepping in to "simplify" matters. How much clearer things would be, they felt, if gold and silver were fixed at a definite ratio, say, twenty ounces of silver to one ounce of gold! Then, both moneys could always circulate at a fixed ratio—and, far more importantly, the government could finally rid itself of the burden of treating money by weight instead of by tale. Let us imagine a unit, the "rur," defined by Ruritanians as 1/20 of an ounce of gold. We have seen how vital it is for the government to induce the public to regard the "rur" as an abstract unit of its own right, only loosely connected to gold. What better way of doing this than to fix the gold/silver ratio? Then, "rur" becomes not only 1/20 ounce of gold, *but also* one ounce of silver. The precise meaning of the word "rur"—a name for gold weight—is now lost, and people begin to think of the "rur" as something tangible in its own right, somehow set by the government, for good and efficient purposes, as equal to certain weights of both gold and silver.

Now we see the importance of abstaining from patriotic or national names for gold ounces or grains. Once such a label replaces the recognized world units of weight, it becomes much easier for governments to manipulate the money unit and give it an apparent life of its own. The fixed gold-silver ration, known as *bimetallism*, accomplished this

task very neatly. It did *not*, however, fulfill its other job of
simplifying the nation's currency. For, once again, Gresham's Law came into prominence. The government usually
set the bimetallic ration originally (say, 20/1) at the going
rate on the free market. But the market ratio, like all market
prices, inevitably changes over time, as supply and demand
conditions change. As changes occur, the fixed bimetallic
ratio inevitably becomes obsolete. Change makes either
gold or silver overvalued. Gold then disappears into cash
balance, black market, or exports, when silver flows in from
abroad and comes out of cash balances to become the only
circulating currency in Ruritania. For centuries, all countries struggled with calamitous effects of suddenly alternat-
ing metallic currencies. First silver would flow in and gold
disappear; then, as the relative market ratios changed, gold
would pour in and silver disappear.[8]

Finally, after weary centuries of bimetallic disruption,
governments picked one metal as the standard, generally
gold. Silver was relegated to "token coin" status, for small
denominations, but not at full weight. (The minting of
token coins was also monopolized by government, and,
since not backed 100 percent by gold, was a means of
expanding the money supply.) The eradication of silver as
money certainly injured many people who preferred to use
silver for various transactions. There was truth in the war-
cry of the bimetallists that a "crime against silver" had been
committed; but the crime was really the original imposition
of bimetallism in lieu of parallel standards. Bimetallism created an impossibly difficult situation, which the government

---

[8]Many debasements, in fact, occurred covertly, with governments claiming
that they were merely bringing the official gold-silver ratio into closer
alignment with the market.

could either meet by going back to full monetary freedom (parallel standards) or by picking one of the two metals as money (gold or silver standard). Full monetary freedom, after all this time, was considered absurd and quixotic; and so the gold standard was generally adopted.

B. *Legal Tender*

How was the government able to enforce its price controls on monetary exchange rates? By a device known as *legal tender laws*. Money is used for payment of past debts, as well as for present "cash" transactions. With the name of the country's currency now prominent in accounting instead its actual weight, contracts began to pledge payment in certain amounts of "money." *Legal tender laws* dictated what that "money" could be. When only the original gold or silver was designated "legal tender," people considered it harmless, but they should have realized that a dangerous precedent had been set for government control of money. If the government sticks to the original money, its legal tender law is superfluous and unnecessary.[9] On the other hand, the government may declare as legal tender a lower-quality currency side-by-side with the original. Thus, the government

---

[9]Lord Farrer, *Studies in Currency 1898* (London: Macmillan, 1898), p. 43.

> The ordinary law of contract does all that is necessary without any law giving special functions to particular forms of currency. We have adopted a gold sovereign as our unit. . . . If I promise to pay 100 sovereigns, it needs no special currency law of legal tender to say that I am bound to pay 100 sovereigns, and that, if required to pay the 100 sovereigns, I cannot discharge my obligation by paying anything else.

On the legal tender laws, see also Ludwig von Mises, *Human Action* (New Haven, Conn.: Yale University Press, 1949), pp. 432n. and 444.

may decree worn coins as good as new ones in paying off debt, or silver and gold equivalent to each other in the fixed ratio. The legal tender laws then bring Gresham's Law into being.

When legal tender laws enshrine an overvalued money, they have another effect; they favor debtors at the expense of creditors. For then debtors are permitted to pay back their debts in a much poorer money than they had borrowed, and creditors are swindled out of the money rightfully theirs. This confiscation of creditors property, however, only benefits outstanding debtors; *future* debtors will be burdened by the scarcity of credit generated by the memory of government spoliation of creditors.

6.
Summary:
Government and Coinage

The compulsory minting monopoly and legal tender legislation were the capstones in governments' drive to gain control of their nations' money. Bolstering these measures, each government moved to abolish the circulation of all coins minted by rival governments.[10] Within each country, only the coin of its own sovereign could now be used; between countries, unstamped gold and silver bullion was used in exchange. This further severed the ties between the various parts of the world market, further sundering one country from another, and disrupting the international division of labor. Yet, purely hard money did not leave too

---

[10]The use of foreign coins was prevalent in the Middle Ages and in the United States down to the middle of the nineteenth century.

much scope for governmental inflation. There were limits to the debasing that governments could engineer, and the fact that all countries used gold and silver placed definite checks on the control of each government over its own territory. The rulers were still held in check by the discipline of an international metallic money.

Governmental control of money could only become absolute, and its counterfeiting unchallenged, as money-substitutes came into prominence in recent centuries. The advent of paper money and bank deposits, an economic boon when backed fully by gold or silver, provided the open sesame for government's road to power over money, and thereby over the entire economic system.

7.
Permitting Banks to Refuse Payment

The modern economy, with its widespread use of banks and money-substitutes, provides the golden opportunity for government to fasten its control over the money supply and permit inflation at its discretion. We have seen in section 12, page 38, that there are three great checks on the power of any bank to inflate under a "free-banking" system: (1) the extent of the clientele of each bank; (2) the extent of the clientele of the whole banking system, i.e., the extent to which people use money-substitutes; and (3) the confidence of the clients in their banks. The narrower the clientele of each bank, of the banking system as a whole, or the shakier the state of confidence, the stricter will be the limits on inflation in the economy. Government's privileging and controlling of the banking system has operated to suspend these limits.

All these limits, of course, rest on one fundamental obligation: the duty of the banks to redeem their sworn liabilities on demand. We have seen that no fractional-reserve bank can redeem all of its liabilities; and we have also seen that this is the gamble that every bank takes. But it is, of course, essential to any system of private property that contract obligations be fulfilled. The bluntest way for government to foster inflation, then, is to grant the banks the special privilege of refusing to pay their obligations, while yet continuing in their operation. While everyone else must pay their debts or go bankrupt, the banks are permitted to refuse redemption of their receipts, at the same time forcing their own debtors to pay when their loans fall due. The usual name for this is a "suspension of specie payments." A more accurate name would be "license for theft;" for what else can we call a governmental permission to continue in business without fulfilling one's contract?

In the United States, mass suspension of specie payment in times of bank troubles became almost a tradition. It started in the War of 1812. Most of the country's banks were located in New England, a section unsympathetic to America's entry into the war. These banks refused to lend for war purposes, and so the government borrowed from new banks in the other states. These banks issued new paper money to make the loans. The inflation was so great that calls for redemption flooded into the new banks, especially from the conservative nonexpanding banks of New England, where the government spent most of its money on war goods. As a result, there was a mass "suspension" in 1814, lasting for over two years (well beyond the end of the war); during that time, banks sprouted up, issuing notes with no need to redeem in gold or silver.

This suspension set a precedent for succeeding economic crises; 1819, 1837, 1857, and so forth. As a result of this tradition, the banks realized that they need have no fear of bankruptcy after an inflation, and this, of course, stimulated inflation and "wildcat banking." Those writers who point to nineteenth century America as a horrid example of "free banking," fail to realize the importance of this clear dereliction of duty by the states in every financial crisis.

The governments and the banks, persuaded the public of the justice of their acts. In fact, anyone trying to get his money back during a crisis was considered "unpatriotic" and a despoiler of his fellowmen, while banks were often commended for patriotically bailing out the community in a time of trouble. Many people, however, were bitter at the entire proceeding and from this sentiment grew the famous "hard money" Jacksonian movement that flourished before the Civil War.[11]

Despite its use in the United States, such periodic privilege to banks did not catch hold as a general policy in the modern world. It was a crude instrument, too sporadic (it could not be permanent since few people would patronize banks that *never* paid their obligations)—and, what's more, it provided no means of government control over the banking system. What governments want, after all, is not simply inflation, but inflation completely controlled and directed by themselves. There must be no danger of the banks running the show. And so, a far subtler, smoother, more permanent method was devised, and sold to the public as a hallmark of civilization itself—Central Banking.

---

[11]See Horace White, *Money and Banking,* 4th ed. (Boston: Ginn, 1911), pp. 322–27.

8.
Central Banking:
Removing the Checks on Inflation

Central Banking is now put in the same class with modern plumbing and good roads: any economy that doesn't have it is called "backward," "primitive," hopelessly out of the swim. America's adoption of the Federal Reserve System—our Central Bank—in 1913 was greeted as finally putting us in the ranks of the "advanced" nations.

Central Banks are often nominally owned by private individuals or, as in the United States, jointly by private banks; but they are always directed by government-appointed officials, and serve as arms of the government. Where they are privately owned, as in the original Bank of England or the Second Bank of the United States, their prospective profits add to the usual governmental desire for inflation.

A Central Bank attains its commanding position from its governmentally granted *monopoly of the note issue.* This is often the unsung key to its power. Invariably, private banks are prohibited from issuing notes, and the privilege is reserved to the Central Bank. The private banks can only grant deposits. If their customers ever wish to shift from deposits to notes, therefore, the banks must go to the Central Bank to get them. Hence the Central Bank's lofty perch as a "bankers' bank." It is a bankers' bank because the bankers are forced to do business with it. As a result, bank deposits became redeemable not only in gold, but also in Central Bank notes. And these new notes were not just plain bank notes. They were liabilities of the Central Bank, an institution invested with all the majestic aura of the government itself. Government, after all, appoints the Bank officials and coordinates its policy with other state policy. It receives the notes in taxes, and declares them to be legal tender.

As a result of these measures, all the banks in the country became clients of the Central Bank.[12] Gold poured into the Central Bank from the private banks, and, in exchange, the public got Central Bank notes and the disuse of gold coins. Gold coins were scoffed at by "official" opinion as cumbersome, old-fashioned, inefficient—an ancient "fetish," perhaps useful in children's socks at Christmas, but that's about all. How much safer, more convenient, more efficient is the gold when resting as bullion in the mighty vaults of the Central Bank! Bathed by this propaganda, and influenced by the convenience and governmental backing of the notes, the public more and more stopped using gold coins in its daily life. Inexorably, the gold flowed into the Central Bank where, more "centralized," it permitted a far greater degree of inflation of money-substitutes.

In the United States, the Federal Reserve Act compels the banks to keep the minimum ratio of reserves to deposits and, since 1917, these reserves could only consist of deposits at the Federal Reserve Bank. Gold could no longer be part of a bank's legal reserves; it had to be deposited in the Federal Reserve Bank.

---

[12]In the United States, the banks were forced by law to join the Federal Reserve System, and to keep their accounts with the Federal Reserve Banks. (Those "state banks" that are not members of the Federal Reserve System keep their reserves with member banks.)

The entire process took the public off the gold habit and placed the people's gold in the none-too-tender care of the State—where it could be confiscated almost painlessly. International traders still used gold bullion in their large-scale transactions, but they were an insignificant proportion of the voting population.

One of the reasons the public could be lured from gold to bank notes was the great *confidence* everyone had in the Central Bank. Surely, the Central Bank, possessed of almost all the gold in the realm, backed by the might and prestige of government, could not fail and go bankrupt! And it is certainly true that no Central Bank in recorded history has ever failed. But why not? Because of the sometimes unwritten but very clear rule that it *could not* be permitted to fail! If governments sometimes allowed private banks to suspend payment, how much more readily would it permit the Central Bank—its own organ—to suspend when in trouble! The precedent was set in Central Banking history when England permitted the Bank of England to suspend in the late eighteenth century, and allowed this suspension for over twenty years.

The Central Bank thus became armed with the almost unlimited confidence of the public. By this time, the public could not see that the Central Bank was being allowed to counterfeit at will, and yet remain immune from any liability if its bona fides should be questioned. It came to see the Central Bank as simply a great national bank, performing a public service, and protected from failure by being a virtual arm of the government.

The Central Bank proceeded to invest the private banks with the public's confidence. This was a more difficult task. The Central Bank let it be known that it would always act as a "lender of last resort" to the banks—i.e., that the Bank would stand ready to lend money to any bank in trouble, especially when many banks are called upon to pay their obligations.

Governments also continued to prop up banks by discouraging bank "runs" (i.e., cases where many clients suspect chicanery and ask to get back their property). Sometimes, they will permitted banks to suspend payment, as in the compulsory bank "holidays" of 1933. Laws were passed prohibiting public encouragement of bank runs, and, as in the 1929 depression in America, government campaigned against "selfish" and "unpatriotic" gold "hoarders." America finally "solved" its pesky problem of bank failures when it adopted Federal Deposit Insurance in 1933. The Federal Deposit Insurance Corporation has only a negligible proportion of "backing" for the bank deposits it "insures." But the public has been given the impression (and one that may well be accurate) that the federal government would stand ready to print enough new money to redeem all of the insured deposits. As a result, the government has managed to transfer its own command of vast public confidence to the entire banking system, as well as to the Central Bank.

We have seen that, by setting up a Central Bank, governments have greatly widened, if not removed, two of the three main checks on bank credit inflation. What of the third check—the problem of the narrowness of each bank's clientele? Removal of this check is one of the main reasons for the Central Bank's existence. In a free-banking system, inflation by any one bank would soon lead to demands for redemption by the other banks, since the clientele of any one bank is severely limited. But the Central Bank, by pumping reserves into all the banks, can make sure that they can all expand together, and at a uniform rate. If all banks are expanding, then there is no redemption problem of one

bank upon another, and each bank finds that its clientele is
really the whole country. In short, the limits on bank expansion are immeasurably widened, from the clientele of each
bank to that of the whole banking system. Of course, this
means that no bank can expand further than the Central
Bank desires. Thus, the government has finally achieved
the power to control and direct the inflation of the banking
system.

In addition to removing the checks on inflation, the act
of establishing a Central Bank has a direct inflationary
impact. Before the Central Bank began, banks kept their
reserves in gold; now gold flows into the Central Bank in
exchange for deposits with the Bank, which are now
reserves for the commercial banks. But the Bank itself keeps
only a fractional reserve of gold to its own liabilities! Therefore, the act of establishing a Central Bank greatly multi-
plies the inflationary potential of the country.[13]

9.
Central Banking:
Directing the Inflation

Precisely how does the Central Bank go about its task of
regulating the private banks? By controlling the banks'

---

[13]The establishment of the Federal Reserve in this way increased three-
fold the expansive power of the banking system of the United States. The
Federal Reserve System also reduced the average legal reserve requirements of all banks from approximately 21 percent in 1913 to 10 percent by
1917, thus further doubling the inflationary potential—a combined potential inflation of six-fold. See Chester A. Phillips, T.F. McManus, and R.W.
Nelson, *Banking and the Business Cycle* (New York: Macmillan, 1937), pp.
23ff.

"reserves"—their deposit accounts at the Central Bank. Banks tend to keep a certain ratio of reserves to their total deposit liabilities, and in the United States government control is made easier by imposing a legal minimum ratio on the bank. The Central Bank can stimulate inflation, then, by pouring reserves into the banking system, and also by lowering the reserve ratio, thus permitting a nationwide bank credit-expansion. If the banks keep a reserve/deposit ratio of 1:10, then "excess reserves" (above the required ratio) of ten million dollars will permit and encourage a nationwide bank inflation of 100 million. Since banks profit by credit expansion, and since government has made it almost impossible for them to fail, they will usually try to keep "loaned up" to their allowable maximum.

The Central Bank adds to the quantity of bank reserves by buying assets on the market. What happens, for example, if the Bank buys an asset (any asset) from Mr. Jones, valued at $1,000? The Central Bank writes out a check to Mr. Jones for $1,000 to pay for the asset. The Central Bank does not keep individual accounts, so Mr. Jones takes the check and deposits it in his bank. Jones' bank credits him with a $1,000 deposit, and presents the check to the Central Bank, which has to credit the bank with an added $1,000 in reserves. This $1,000 in reserves permits a multiple bank credit expansion, particularly if added reserves are in this way poured into many banks across the country.

If the Central Bank buys an asset from a bank directly, then the result is even clearer; the bank adds to its reserves, and a base for multiple credit expansion is established.

Undoubtedly, the favorite asset for Central Bank purchase has been government securities. In that way, the government assures a market for its own securities. Government can easily inflate the money supply by issuing new bonds, and then order its Central Bank to purchase them. Often the Central Bank undertakes to support the market price of government securities at a certain level, thereby causing a flow of securities into the Bank, and a consequent perpetual inflation.

Besides buying assets, the Central Bank can create new bank reserves in another way: by lending them. The rate which the Central Bank charges the banks for this service is the "rediscount rate." Clearly, borrowed reserves are not as satisfactory to the banks as reserves that are wholly theirs, since there is now pressure for repayment. Changes in the rediscount rate receive a great deal of publicity, but they are clearly of minor importance compared to the movements in the quantity of bank reserves and the reserve ratio.

When the Central Bank sells assets to the banks or the public, it lowers bank reserves, and causes pressure for credit contraction and deflation—lowering—of the money supply. We have seen, however, that governments are inherently inflationary; historically, deflationary action by the government has been negligible and fleeting. One thing is often forgotten: deflation can only take place after a previous inflation; only pseudo-receipts, not gold coins, can be retired and liquidated.

10.
Going Off the Gold Standard

The establishment of Central Banking removes the checks of bank credit expansion, and puts the inflationary engine into operation. It does not remove all restraints, however. There is still the problem of the Central Bank itself. The citizens can conceivably make a run on the Central Bank, but this is most improbable. A more formidable threat is the loss of gold to foreign nations. For just as the expansion of one bank loses gold to the clients of other, nonexpanding banks, so does monetary expansion in one country cause a loss of gold to the citizens of other countries. Countries that expand faster are in danger of gold losses and calls upon their banking system for gold redemption. This was the classic cyclical pattern of the nineteenth century; a country's Central Bank would generate bank credit expansion; prices would rise; and as the new money spread from domestic to foreign clientele, foreigners would more and more try to redeem the currency in gold. Finally, the Central Bank would have to call a halt and enforce a credit contraction in order to save the monetary standard.

There is one way that foreign redemption can be avoided: inter-Central Bank cooperation. If all Central Banks agree to inflate at about the same rate, then no country would lose gold to any other, and all the world together could inflate almost without limit. With every government jealous of its own power and responsive to different pressures, however, such goose-step cooperation has so far proved almost impossible. One of the closest approaches was the American Federal Reserve agreement to promote domestic inflation in the 1920s in order to help Great Britain and prevent it from losing gold to the United States.

In the twentieth century, governments, rather than deflate or limit their own inflation, have simply "gone off the gold standard" when confronted with heavy demands for gold. This, of course, insures that the Central Bank cannot fail, since its notes now become the standard money. In short, government has finally refused to pay its debts, and has virtually absolved the banking system from that onerous duty. Pseudo-receipts to gold were first issued without backing and then, when the day of reckoning drew near, the bankruptcy was shamelessly completed by simply eliminating gold redemption. The severance of the various national currency names (dollar, pound, mark) from gold and silver is now complete.

At first, governments refused to admit that this was a permanent measure. They referred to the "suspension of specie payments," and it was always understood that eventually, after the war or other "emergency" had ended, the government would again redeem its obligations. When the Bank of England went off gold at the end of the eighteenth century, it continued in this state for twenty years, but always with the understanding that gold payment would be resumed after the French wars were ended.

Temporary "suspensions," however, are primrose paths to outright repudiation. The gold standard, after all, is no spigot that can be turned on or off as government whim decrees. Either a gold-receipt is redeemable or it is not; once redemption is suspended the gold standard is itself a mockery.

Another step in the slow extinction of gold money was the establishment of the "gold bullion standard." Under this system, the currency is no longer redeemable in coins; it can only be redeemed in large, highly valuable, gold bars. This, in effect, limits gold redemption to a handful of specialists in foreign trade. There is no longer a true gold standard, but governments can still proclaim their adherence to gold. The European "gold standards" of the 1920s were pseudo-standards of this type.[14]

---

[14]See Melchior Palyi, "The Meaning of the Gold Standard," *Journal of Business* (July 1941): 299–304.

Finally, governments went "off gold" officially and completely, in a thunder of abuse against foreigners and "unpatriotic gold hoarders." Government paper now becomes the *fiat* standard money. Sometimes, Treasury rather than Central Bank paper has been the fiat money, especially before the development of a Central Banking system. The American Continentals, the Greenbacks, and Confederate notes of the Civil War period, the French *assignats*, were all fiat currencies issued by the Treasuries. But whether Treasury or Central Bank, the effect of fiat issue is the same: the monetary standard is now at the mercy of the government, and bank deposits are redeemable simply in government paper.

11.
Fiat Money and the Gold Problem

When a country goes off the gold standard and onto the fiat standard, it adds to the number of "moneys" in existence. In addition to the commodity moneys, gold and silver, there now flourish independent moneys directed by each government imposing its fiat rule. And just as gold and silver will have an exchange rate on the free market, so the market will establish exchange rates for all the various moneys. In a world of fiat moneys, each currency, if permitted, will fluctuate freely in relation to all the others. We have seen that for any two moneys, the exchange rate is set in accordance with the proportionate purchasing-power parities, and that these in turn are determined by the respective supplies and demands for the various currencies. When a currency changes its character from gold-receipt to fiat paper, confidence in its stability and quality is shaken, and demand for it declines. Furthermore, now that it is cut off from gold, its far greater quantity relative to its former gold backing now becomes evident. With a supply greater than gold and a lower demand, its purchasing-power, and hence its exchange rate, quickly depreciate in relation to gold. And since government is inherently inflationary, it will keep depreciating as time goes on.

Such depreciation is highly embarrassing to the government—and hurts citizens who try to import goods. The existence of gold in the economy is a constant reminder of the poor quality of the government paper, and it always poses a threat to replace the paper as the country's money. Even with the government giving all the backing of its prestige and its legal tender laws to its fiat paper, gold coins in the hands of the public will always be a permanent reproach and menace to the government's power over the country's money.

In America's first depression, 1819–1821, four Western states (Tennessee, Kentucky, Illinois, and Missouri) established state-owned banks, issuing fiat paper. They were backed by legal tender provisions in the states, and sometimes by legal prohibition against depreciating the notes. And yet, all these experiments, born in high hopes, came quickly to grief as the new paper depreciated rapidly to negligible value. The projects had to be swiftly abandoned. Later, the greenbacks circulated as fiat paper in the North during and after the Civil War. Yet, in California, the people refused to accept the greenbacks and continued to use gold as their money. As a prominent economist pointed out:

> In California, as in other states, the paper was legal tender and was receivable for public dues; nor was there any distrust or hostility toward the federal government. But there was a strong feeling . . . in favor of gold and against paper. . . . Every debtor

had the legal right to pay off his debts in depreciated paper. But if he did so, he was a marked man
(the creditor was likely to post him publicly in the
newspapers) and he was virtually boycotted.
Throughout this period paper was not used in California. The people of the state conducted their
transactions in gold, while all the rest of the United
States used convertible paper.[15]

It became clear to governments that they could not
afford to allow people to own and keep their gold. Government could never cement its power over a nation's currency,
if the people, when in need, could repudiate the fiat paper
and turn to gold for their money. Accordingly, governments
have outlawed gold holding by their citizens. Gold, except
for a negligible amount permitted for industrial and orna-
mental purposes, has generally been nationalized. To ask
for return of the public's confiscated property is now considered hopelessly backward and old-fashioned.[16]

12.
Fiat Money and Gresham's Law

With fiat money established and gold outlawed, the
way is clear for full-scale, government-run inflation. Only

---

[15]Frank W. Taussig, *Principles of Economics*, 2nd ed. (New York: Macmillan, 1916), vol. I, p. 312. Also see J.K. Upton, *Money in Politics*, 2nd ed.
(Boston: Lothrop Publishing, 1895), pp. 69 ff.

[16]For an incisive analysis of the steps by which the American government
confiscated the people's gold and went off the gold standard in 1933, see
Garet Garrett, *The People's Pottage* (Caldwell, Idaho: Caxton Printers,
1953), pp. 15–41.

one very broad check remains: the ultimate threat of hyper-inflation, the crack-up of the currency. Hyper-inflation occurs when the public realizes that the government is bent on inflation, and decides to evade the inflationary tax on its resources by spending money as fast as possible while it still retains some value. Until hyper-inflation sets in, however, government can now manage the currency and the inflation undisturbed. New difficulties arise, however. As always, government intervention to cure one problem raises a host of new, unexpected problems. In a world of fiat moneys, each country has its own money. The international division of labor, based on an international currency, has been broken, and countries tend to divide into their own autarchic units. Lack of monetary certainty disrupts trade further. The standard of living in each country thereby declines. Each country has freely-fluctuating exchange rates with all other currencies. A country inflating beyond the others no longer fears a loss of gold; but it faces other unpleasant consequences. The exchange rate of its currency falls in relation to foreign currencies. This is not only embarrassing but even disturbing to citizens who fear further depreciation. It also greatly raises the costs of imported goods, and this means a great deal to those countries with a high proportion of international trade.

In recent years, therefore, governments have moved to abolish freely-fluctuating exchange rates. Instead, they fixed arbitrary exchange rates with other currencies. Gresham's Law tells us precisely the result of any such arbitrary price control. Whatever rate is set will not be the free-market one, since that can be only be determined from day-to-day on the market. Therefore, one currency will always be artificially overvalued and the other, undervalued. Generally, governments have deliberately overvalued their currencies—for prestige reasons, and also because of the consequences that follow. When a currency is overvalued by decree, people rush to exchange it for the undervalued currency at the bargain rates; this causes a surplus of overvalued, and a shortage of the undervalued, currency. The rate, in short, is prevented from moving to clear the exchange market. In the present world, foreign currencies have generally been overvalued relative to the dollar. The result has been the famous phenomenon of the "dollar shortage"—another testimony to the operation of Gresham's Law.

Foreign countries, clamoring about a "dollar shortage," thus brought it about by their own policies. It is possible that these governments actually welcomed this state of affairs, for (a) it gave them an excuse to clamor for American dollar aid to "relieve the dollar shortage in the free world," and (b) it gave them an excuse to ration imports from America. Undervaluing dollars causes imports from America to be artificially cheap and exports to America artifically expensive. The result: a trade deficit and worry over the dollar drain.[17] The foreign government then stepped in to tell its people sadly that it is unfortunately necessary for it to ration imports: to issue licenses to importers, and determine what is imported "according to need." To ration imports, many governments confiscate the foreign exchange holdings of their citizens, backing up an artificially high valuation on domestic currency by forcing these citizens to accept far less domestic money than they could have acquired on the free market. Thus, foreign exchange, as well as gold, has been nationalized, and

---

[17]In the last few years, the dollar has been overvalued in relation to other currencies, and hence the dollar drains *from* the U.S.

exporters penalized. In countries where foreign trade is vitally important, this government "exchange control" imposes virtual socialization on the economy. An artificial exchange rate thus gives countries an excuse for demanding foreign aid and for imposing socialist controls over trade.[18]

At present, the world is enmeshed in a chaotic welter of exchange controls, currency blocs, restrictions on convertibility, and multiple systems of rates. In some countries a "black market" in foreign exchange is legally encouraged to find out the true rate, and multiple discriminatory rates are fixed for different types of transactions. Almost all nations are on a fiat standard, but they have not had the courage to admit this outright, and so they proclaim some such fiction as "restricted gold bullion standard." Actually, gold is used not as a true definition for currencies, but as a convenience by governments: for (a) fixing a currency's rate with respect to gold makes it easy to reckon any exchange in terms of any other currency; and (b) gold is still used by the different governments. Since exchange rates are fixed, *some* item must move to balance every country's payments, and gold is the ideal candidate. In short gold is no longer the world's money; it is now the *governments'* money, used in payments to one another.

Clearly, the inflationists' dream is some sort of world paper money, manipulated by a world government and Central Bank, inflating everywhere at a common rate. This dream still lies in the dim future, however; we are still far from world government, and national currency problems

---

[18]For an excellent discussion of foreign exchange and exchange controls, see George Winder, *The Free Convertibility of Sterling* (London: Batchworth Press, 1955).

have so far been too diverse and conflicting to permit meshing into a single unit. Yet, the world has moved steadily in this direction. The International Monetary Fund, for example, is basically an institution designed to bolster national exchange control in general, and foreign undervaluation of the dollar in particular. The Fund requires each member country to fix its exchange rate, and then to pool gold and dollars to lend to governments that find themselves short of hard currency.

13.
Government and Money

Many people believe that the free market, despite some admitted advantages, is a picture of disorder and chaos. Nothing is "planned," everything is haphazard. Government dictation, on the other hand, seems simple and orderly; decrees are handed down and they are obeyed. In no area of the economy is this myth more prevalent than in the field of money. Seemingly, money, at least, must come under stringent government control. But money is the lifeblood of the economy; it is the medium for all transactions. If government dictates over money, it has already captured a vital command post for control over the economy, and has secured a stepping-stone for full socialism. We have seen that a free market in money, contrary to common assumption, would not be chaotic; that, in fact, it would be a model of order and efficiency.

What, then, have we learned about government and money? We have seen that, over the centuries, government has, step by step, invaded the free market and seized complete control over the monetary system. We have seen that each new control, sometimes seemingly innocuous, has begotten new and further controls. We have seen that governments are inherently inflationary, since inflation is a tempting means of acquiring revenue for the State and its favored groups. The slow but certain seizure of the monetary reins has thus been used to (a) inflate the economy at a pace decided by government; and (b) bring about socialistic direction of the entire economy.

Furthermore, government meddling with money has not only brought untold tyranny into the world; it has also brought chaos and not order. It has fragmented the peaceful, productive world market and shattered it into a thousand pieces, with trade and investment hobbled and hampered by myriad restrictions, controls, artificial rates, currency breakdowns, etc. It has helped bring about wars by transforming a world of peaceful intercourse into a jungle of warring currency blocs. In short, we find that coercion, in money as in other matters, brings, not order, but conflict and chaos.

IV.

THE MONETARY BREAKDOWN
OF THE WEST

SINCE THE FIRST EDITION OF this book was written, the chickens of the monetary interventionists have come home to roost. The world monetary crisis of February–March, 1973, followed by the dollar plunge of July, was only the latest of an accelerating series of crises which provide a virtual textbook illustration of our analysis of the inevitable consequences of government intervention in the monetary system. After each crisis is temporarily allayed by a "Band-Aid" solution, the governments of the West loudly announce that the world monetary system has now been placed on sure footing, and that all the monetary crises have been solved. President Nixon went so far as to call the Smithsonian Agreement of December 18, 1971, the "greatest monetary agreement in the history of the world," only to see this greatest agreement collapse in a little over a year. Each "solution" has crumbled more rapidly than its predecessor.

97

To understand the current monetary chaos, it is necessary to trace briefly the international monetary developments of the twentieth century, and to see how each set of unsound inflationist interventions has collapsed of its own inherent problems, only to set the stage for another round of interventions. The twentieth century history of the world monetary order can be divided into nine phases. Let us examine each in turn.

1.

Phase I:
The Classical Gold Standard, 1815–1914

We can look back upon the "classical" gold standard, the Western world of the nineteenth and early twentieth centuries, as the literal and metaphorical Golden Age. With the exception of the troublesome problem of silver, the world was on a gold standard, which meant that each national currency (the dollar, pound, franc, etc.) was merely a *name* for a certain definite *weight* of gold. The "dollar," for example, was defined as 1/20 of a gold ounce, the pound sterling as slightly less than 1/4 of a gold ounce, and so on. This meant that the "exchange rates" between the various national currencies were fixed, not because they were arbitrarily controlled by government, but in the same way that one pound of weight is defined as being equal to sixteen ounces.

The international gold standard meant that the benefits of having one money medium were extended throughout the world. One of the reasons for the growth and prosperity of the United States has been the fact that we have enjoyed *one* money throughout the large area of the country. We have had a gold or at least a single dollar standard within the entire country, and did not have to suffer the chaos of each city and county issuing its own money which would then fluctuate with respect to the moneys of all the other cities and counties. The nineteenth century saw the benefits of one money throughout the civilized world. One money facilitated freedom of trade, investment, and travel throughout that trading and monetary area, with the consequent growth of specialization and the international division of labor.

It must be emphasized that gold was not selected arbitrarily by governments to be the monetary standard. Gold had developed for many centuries on the free market as the best money; as the commodity providing the most stable and desirable monetary medium. Above all, the supply and provision of gold was subject only to market forces, and not to the arbitrary printing press of the government.

The international gold standard provided an automatic market mechanism for checking the inflationary potential of government. It also provided an automatic mechanism for keeping the balance of payments of each country in equilibrium. As the philosopher and economist David Hume pointed out in the mid-eighteenth century, if one nation, say France, inflates its supply of paper francs, its prices rise; the increasing incomes in paper francs stimulate imports from abroad, which are also spurred by the fact that prices of imports are now relatively cheaper than prices at home. At the same time, the higher prices at home discourage exports abroad; the result is a deficit in the balance of payments, which must be paid for by foreign countries cashing in francs for gold. The gold outflow means that France must eventually contract its inflated paper francs in order to prevent a loss of all of its gold. If the inflation has taken the form of bank deposits, then the French banks have to contract their loans and deposits in order to avoid bankruptcy as foreigners call upon the French banks to redeem their deposits in gold. The contraction lowers prices at home, and generates an export surplus, thereby reversing the gold outflow, until the price levels are equalized in France and in other countries as well.

It is true that the interventions of governments previous to the nineteenth century weakened the speed of this market mechanism, and allowed for a business cycle of inflation and recession within this gold standard framework. These interventions were particularly: the governments' monopolizing of the mint, legal tender laws, the creation of paper money, and the development of inflationary banking propelled by each of the governments. But while these interventions slowed the adjustments of the market, these adjustments were still in ultimate control of the situation. So while the classical gold standard of the nineteenth century was not perfect, and allowed for relatively minor booms and busts, it still provided us with by far the best monetary order the world has ever known, an order which worked, which kept business cycles from getting out of hand, and which enabled the development of free international trade, exchange, and investment.[1]

---

[1]For a recent study of the classical gold standard, and a history of the early phases of its breakdown in the twentieth century, see Melchior Palyi, *The Twilight of Gold, 1914–1936* (Chicago: Henry Regnery, 1972).

2.

Phase II:
World War I and After

If the classical gold standard worked so well, why did it break down? It broke down because governments were entrusted with the task of keeping their monetary promises, of seeing to it that pounds, dollars, francs, etc., were always redeemable in gold as they and their controlled banking system had pledged. It was not gold that failed; it was the folly of trusting government to keep its promises. To wage the catastrophic war of World War I, each government had to inflate its own supply of paper and bank currency. So severe was this inflation that it was impossible for the warring governments to keep their pledges, and so they went "off the gold standard," i.e., declared their own bankruptcy, shortly after entering the war. All except the United States, which entered the war late, and did not inflate the supply of dollars enough to endanger redeemability. But, apart from the United States, the world suffered what some economists now hail as the Nirvana of freely-fluctuating exchange rates (now called "dirty floats") competitive devaluations, warring currency blocs, exchange controls, tariffs and quotas, and the breakdown of international trade and investment. The inflated pounds, francs, marks, etc., depreciated in relation to gold and the dollar; monetary chaos abounded throughout the world.

In those days there were, happily, very few economists to hail this situation as the monetary ideal. It was generally recognized that Phase II was the threshold to international disaster, and politicians and economists looked around for ways to restore the stability and freedom of the classical gold standard.

3.

Phase III:
The Gold Exchange Standard
(Britain and the United States) 1926–1931

How to return to the Golden Age? The sensible thing to do would have been to recognize the facts of reality, the fact of the depreciated pound, franc, mark, etc., and to return to the gold standard at a redefined rate: a rate that would recognize the existing supply of money and price levels. The British pound, for example, had been traditionally defined at a weight which made it equal to $4.86. But by the end of World War I, the inflation in Britain had brought the pound down to approximately $3.50 on the free foreign exchange market. Other currencies were similarly depreciated. The sensible policy would have been for Britain to return to gold at approximately $3.50, and for the other inflated countries to do the same. Phase I could have been smoothly and rapidly restored. Instead, the British made the fateful decision to return to gold at the old par of $4.86.[2] It did so for reasons of British national "prestige," and in a vain attempt to re-establish London as the "hard money" financial center of the world. To succeed at this piece of heroic folly, Britain would have had to deflate severely its money supply and its price levels, for at a $4.86 pound British export prices were

---

[2]On the crucial British error and its consequence in leading to the 1929 depression, see Lionel Robbins, *The Great Depression* (New York: Macmillan, 1934).

far too high to be competitive in the world markets. But deflation was now politically out of the question, for the growth of trade unions, buttressed by a nationwide system of unemployment insurance, had made wage rates rigid downward; in order to deflate, the British government would have had to reverse the growth of its welfare state. In fact, the British wished to continue to inflate money and prices. As a result of combining inflation with a return to an overvalued par, British exports were depressed all during the 1920s and unemployment was severe all during the period when most of the world was experiencing an economic boom.

How could the British try to have their cake and eat it at the same time? By establishing a new international monetary order which would induce or coerce *other* governments into inflating or into going back to gold at overvalued pars for their *own* currencies, thus crippling their own exports and subsidizing imports from Britain. This is precisely what Britain did, as it led the way, at the Genoa Conference of 1922, in creating a new international monetary order, the gold-exchange standard.

The gold-exchange standard worked as follows: The United States remained on the classical gold standard, redeeming dollars in gold. Britain and the other countries of the West, however, returned to a pseudo-gold standard, Britain in 1926 and the other countries around the same time. British pounds and other currencies were not payable in gold coins, but only in large-sized bars, suitable only for international transactions. This prevented the ordinary citizens of Britain and other European countries from using gold in their daily life, and thus permitted a wider degree of paper and bank inflation. But furthermore, Britain redeemed pounds not merely in gold, but also in dollars;

while the other countries redeemed their currencies not in gold, but in pounds. And most of these countries were induced by Britain to return to gold at overvalued parities. The result was a pyramiding of United States on gold, of British pounds on dollars, and of other European currencies on pounds—the "gold-exchange standard," with the dollar and the pound as the two "key currencies."

Now when Britain inflated, and experienced a deficit in its balance of payments, the gold standard mechanism did not work to quickly restrict British inflation. For instead of other countries redeeming their pounds for gold, they kept the pounds and inflated on top of them. Hence Britain and Europe were permitted to inflate unchecked, and British deficits could pile up unrestrained by the market discipline of the gold standard. As for the United States, Britain was able to induce the United States to inflate dollars so as not to lose many dollar reserves or gold to the United States.

The point of the gold-exchange standard is that it cannot last; the piper must eventually be paid, but only in a disastrous reaction to the lengthy inflationary boom. As sterling balances piled up in France, the United States, and elsewhere, the slightest loss of confidence in the increasingly shaky and jerry-built inflationary structure was bound to lead to general collapse. This is precisely what happened in 1931; the failure of inflated banks throughout Europe, and the attempt of "hard money" France to cash in its sterling balances for gold, led Britain to go off the gold standard completely. Britain was soon followed by the other countries of Europe.

4.

Phase IV:
Fluctuating Fiat Currencies, 1931–1945

The world was now back to the monetary chaos of World War I, except that now there seemed to be little hope for a restoration of gold. The international economic order had disintegrated into the chaos of clean and dirty floating exchange rates, competing devaluations, exchange controls, and trade barriers; international economic and monetary warfare raged between currencies and currency blocs. International trade and investment came to a virtual standstill; and trade was conducted through barter agreements conducted by governments competing and conflicting with one another. Secretary of State Cordell Hull repeatedly pointed out that these monetary and economic conflicts of the 1930s were the major cause of World War II.[3]

The United States remained on the gold standard for two years, and then, in 1933–34, went off the classical gold standard in a vain attempt to get out of the depression. American citizens could no longer redeem dollars in gold, and were even prohibited from owning any gold, either here or abroad. But the United States remained, after 1934, on a peculiar new form of gold standard, in which the dollar, now redefined to 1/35 of a gold ounce, was redeemable in gold to foreign governments and Central Banks. A lingering tie to gold remained. Furthermore, the monetary chaos in

---

[3]Cordell Hull, *Memoirs* (New York, 1948), vol. I, p. 81. Also see Richard N. Gardner, *Sterling-Dollar Conspiracy* (Oxford: Clarendon Press, 1956), p. 141.

Europe led to gold flowing into the only relatively safe monetary haven, the United States.

The chaos and the unbridled economic warfare of the 1930s points up an important lesson: the grievous *political* flaw (apart from the economic problems) in the Milton Friedman-Chicago School monetary scheme for freely-fluctuating fiat currencies. For what the Friedmanites would do—*in the name of the free market*—is to cut all ties to gold completely, leave the absolute control of each national currency in the hands of its central government issuing fiat paper as legal tender—*and then* advise each government to allow its currency to fluctuate freely with respect to all other fiat currencies, as well as to refrain from inflating its currency too outrageously. The grave political flaw is to hand total control of the money supply to the Nation-State, and then to hope and expect that the State will refrain from using that power. And since power always tends to be used, including the power to counterfeit legally, the naivete, as well as the statist nature, of this type of program should be starkly evident.

And so, the disastrous experience of Phase IV, the 1930s world of fiat paper and economic warfare, led the United States authorities to adopt as their major economic war aim of World War II the restoration of a viable international monetary order, an order on which could be built a renaissance of world trade and the fruits of the international division of labor.

5.

Phase V:
Bretton Woods and the New Gold
Exchange Standard (the United States)
1945–1968

The new international monetary order was conceived and then driven through by the United States at an international monetary conference at Bretton Woods, New Hampshire, in mid-1944, and ratified by the Congress in July, 1945. While the Bretton Woods system worked far better than the disaster of the 1930s, it worked only as another inflationary recrudescence of the gold-exchange standard of the 1920s and—like the 1920s—the system lived only on borrowed time.

The new system was essentially the gold-exchange standard of the 1920s but with the dollar rudely displacing the British pound as one of the "key currencies." Now the dollar, valued at 1/35 of a gold ounce, was to be the *only* key currency. The other difference from the 1920s was that the dollar was no longer redeemable in gold to American citizens; instead, the 1930's system was continued, with the dollar redeemable in gold *only* to foreign governments and their Central Banks. No private individuals, only governments, were to be allowed the privilege of redeeming dollars in the world gold currency. In the Bretton Woods system, the United States pyramided dollars (in paper money and in bank deposits) on top of gold, in which dollars could be redeemed by foreign governments; while all other governments held dollars as their basic reserve and pyramided their currency on top of dollars. And since the United States began the post-war world with a huge stock of gold (approximately $25 billion) there was plenty of play for pyramiding dollar claims on top of it. Furthermore, the system could "work" for a while because all the world's currencies returned to the new system at their pre-World War II pars, most of which were highly overvalued in terms of their inflated and depreciated currencies. The inflated pound sterling, for example, returned at $4.86, even though it was worth far less than that in terms of purchasing power on the market. Since the dollar was artificially undervalued and most other currencies overvalued in 1945, the dollar was made scarce, and the world suffered from a so-called dollar shortage, which the American taxpayer was supposed to be obligated to make up by foreign aid. In short, the export surplus enjoyed by the undervalued American dollar was to be partly financed by the hapless American taxpayer in the form of foreign aid.

There being plenty of room for inflation before retribution could set in, the United States government embarked on its post-war policy of continual monetary inflation, a policy it has pursued merrily ever since. By the early 1950s, the continuing American inflation began to turn the tide of international trade. For while the United States was inflating and expanding money and credit, the major European governments, many of them influenced by "Austrian" monetary advisers, pursued a relatively "hard money" policy (e.g., West Germany, Switzerland, France, Italy). Steeply inflationist Britain was compelled by its outflow of dollars to devalue the pound to more realistic levels (for a while it was approximately $2.40). All this, combined with the increasing productivity of Europe, and later Japan, led to continuing balance of payments deficits with the United States. As the 1950s and 1960s wore on, the United States became more and more inflationist, both absolutely and relatively to Japan and Western Europe. But the classical gold standard check on inflation—especially *American* inflation—was gone. For the rules of the Bretton Woods game provided that the West European countries had to keep piling up their reserve, and even use these dollars as a base to inflate their own currency and credit.

But as the 1950s and 1960s continued, the harder-money countries of West Europe (and Japan) became restless at being forced to pile up dollars that were now increasingly overvalued instead of undervalued. As the purchasing power and hence the true value of dollars fell, they became increasingly unwanted by foreign governments. But they were locked into a system that was more and more of a nightmare. The American reaction to the European complaints, headed by France and DeGaulle's major monetary adviser, the classical gold-standard economist Jacques Rueff, was merely scorn and brusque dismissal. American politicians and economists simply declared that Europe was *forced* to use the dollar as its currency, that it could do nothing about its growing problems, and therefore the United States could keep blithely inflating while pursuing a policy of "benign neglect" toward the international monetary consequences of its own actions.

But Europe did have the legal option of redeeming dollars in gold at $35 an ounce. And as the dollar became increasingly overvalued in terms of hard money currencies and gold, European governments began more and more to exercise that option. The gold standard check was coming into use; hence gold flowed steadily out of the United States for two decades after the early 1950s, until the United States gold stock dwindled over this period from over $20 billion to $9 billion. As dollars kept inflating upon a dwindling gold base, how could the United States keep redeeming foreign dollars in gold—the cornerstone of the Bretton Woods system? These problems did not slow down continued United States inflation of dollars and prices, or the United States policy of "benign neglect," which resulted by the late 1960s in an accelerated pileup of no less than $80 billion in unwanted dollars in Europe (known as Eurodollars). To try to stop European redemption of dollars into gold, the United States exerted intense political pressure on the European governments, similar but on a far larger scale to the British cajoling of France not to redeem its heavy sterling balances until 1931. But economic law has a way, at long last, of catching up with governments, and this is what happened to the inflation-happy United States government by the end of the 1960s. The gold-exchange system of Bretton Woods—hailed by the United States political and economic Establishment as permanent and impregnable—began to unravel rapidly in 1968.

6.
Phase VI:
The Unraveling of Bretton Woods,
1968–1971

As dollars piled up abroad and gold continued to flow outward, the United States found it increasingly difficult to maintain the price of gold at $35 an ounce in the free gold markets at London and Zurich. Thirty-five dollars an ounce was the keystone of the system, and while American citizens have been barred since 1934 from owning gold anywhere in the world, other citizens have enjoyed the freedom to own gold bullion and coin. Hence, one way for individual Europeans to redeem their dollars in gold was to sell their dollars for gold at \$35 an ounce in the free gold market. As the dollar kept inflating and depreciating, and as American balance of payments deficits continued, Europeans and other private citizens began to accelerate their sales of dollars into gold. In order to keep the dollar at \$35 an ounce, the United States government was forced to leak out gold from its dwindling stock to support the \$35 price at London and Zurich.

A crisis of confidence in the dollar on the free gold markets led the United States to effect a fundamental change in the monetary system in March 1968. The idea was to stop the pesky free gold market from ever again endangering the Bretton Woods arrangement. Hence was born the "two-tier gold market." The idea was that the free gold market could go to blazes; it would be strictly insulated from the *real* monetary action in the Central Banks and governments of the world. The United States would no longer try to keep the free-market gold price at \$35; it would ignore the free gold market, and it and all the other governments agreed to keep the value of the dollar at \$35 an ounce forevermore. The governments and Central Banks of the world would henceforth buy no more gold from the "outside" market and would sell no more gold to that market; from now on gold would simply move as counters from one Central Bank to another, and new gold supplies, free gold market, or private demand for gold would take their own course completely separated from the monetary arrangements of the world.

Along with this, the United States pushed hard for the new launching of a new kind of world paper reserve, Special Drawing Rights (SDRs), which it was hoped would eventually replace gold altogether and serve as a new world paper currency to be issued by a future World Reserve

Bank; if such a system were ever established, then the United States could inflate unchecked forevermore, in collaboration with other world governments (the only limit would then be the disastrous one of a worldwide runaway inflation and the crackup of the world paper currency). But the SDRs, combatted intensely as they have been by Western Europe and the "hard-money" countries, have so far been only a small supplement to American and other currency reserves.

All pro-paper economists, from Keynesians to Friedmanites, were now confident that gold would disappear from the international monetary system; cut off from its "support" by the dollar, these economists all confidently predicted, the free-market gold price would soon fall below $35 an ounce, and even down to the estimated "industrial" nonmonetary gold price of $10 an ounce. Instead, the free price of gold, never below $35, had been steadily above $35, and by early 1973 had climbed to around $125 an ounce, a figure that no pro-paper economist would have thought possible as recently as a year earlier.

Far from establishing a permanent new monetary system, the two-tier gold market only bought a few years of time; American inflation and deficits continued. Eurodollars accumulated rapidly, gold continued to flow outward, and the higher free-market price of gold simply revealed the accelerated loss of world confidence in the dollar. The two-tier system moved rapidly toward crisis—and to the final dissolution of Bretton Woods.[4]

---

[4]On the two-tier gold market, see Jacques Rueff, *The Monetary Sin of the West* (New York: Macmillan, 1972).

7.
Phase VII:
The End of Bretton Woods:
Fluctuating Fiat Currencies,
August–December 1971

On August 15, 1971, at the same time that President Nixon imposed a price-wage freeze in a vain attempt to check bounding inflation, Mr. Nixon also brought the post-war Bretton Woods system to a crashing end. As European Central Banks at last threatened to redeem much of their swollen stock of dollars for gold, President Nixon went totally off gold. For the first time in American history, the dollar was totally fiat, totally without backing in gold. Even the tenuous link with gold maintained since 1933 was now severed. The world was plunged into the fiat system of the thirties—and worse, since now even the dollar was no longer linked to gold. Ahead loomed the dread spectre of currency blocs, competing devaluations, economic warfare, and the breakdown of international trade and investment, with the worldwide depression that would then ensue.

What to do? Attempting to restore an international monetary order lacking a link to gold, the United States led the world into the Smithsonian Agreement on December 18, 1971.

8.

Phase VIII:
The Smithsonian Agreement,
December 1971–February 1973

The Smithsonian Agreement, hailed by President Nixon as the "greatest monetary agreement in the history of the world," was even more shaky and unsound than the gold-exchange standard of the 1920s or than Bretton Woods. For once again, the countries of the world pledged to maintain fixed exchange rates, but this time with no gold or world money to give any currency backing. Furthermore, many European currencies were fixed at undervalued parities in relation to the dollar; the only United States concession was a puny devaluation of the official dollar rate to $38 an ounce. But while much too little and too late, this devaluation was significant in violating an endless round of official American pronouncements, which had pledged to maintain the $35 rate forevermore. Now at last the $35 price was implicitly acknowledged as not graven on tablets of stone.

It was inevitable that fixed exchange rates, even with wider agreed zones of fluctuation, but lacking a world medium of exchange, were doomed to rapid defeat. This was especially true since American inflation of money and prices, the decline of the dollar, and balance of payments deficits continued unchecked.

The swollen supply of Eurodollars, combined with the continued inflation and the removal of gold backing, drove the free-market gold price up to $215 an ounce. And as the overvaluation of the dollar and the undervaluation of European and Japanese hard money became increasingly evident, the dollar finally broke apart on the world markets in the panic months of February–March 1973. It became impossible for West Germany, Switzerland, France and the other hard money countries to continue to buy dollars in order to support the dollar at an overvalued rate. In little over a year, the Smithsonian system of fixed exchange rates without gold had smashed apart on the rocks of economic reality.

9.
Phase IX:
Fluctuating Fiat Currencies,
March 1973–?

With the dollar breaking apart, the world shifted again, to a system of fluctuating fiat currencies. Within the West European bloc, exchange rates were tied to one another, and the United States again devalued the official dollar rate by a token amount to $42 an ounce. As the dollar plunged in foreign exchange from day to day, and the West German mark, the Swiss franc, and the Japanese yen hurtled upward, the American authorities, backed by the Friedmanite economists, began to think that this was the monetary ideal. It is true that dollar surpluses and sudden balance of payments crises do not plague the world under fluctuating exchange rates. Furthermore, American export firms began to chortle that falling dollar rates made American goods cheaper abroad, and therefore benefitted exports. It is true that governments persisted in interfering with exchange fluctuations ("dirty" instead of "clean" floats), but overall it seemed that the international monetary order had sundered into a Friedmanite utopia.

But it became clear all too soon that all is far from well in the current international monetary system. The long-run problem is that the hard-money countries will not sit by forever and watch their currencies become more expensive and their exports hurt for the benefit of their American competitors. If American inflation and dollar depreciation continues, they will soon shift to the competing devaluation, exchange controls, currency blocs, and economic warfare of the 1930s. But more immediate is the other side of the coin: the fact that depreciating dollars means that American imports are far more expensive, American tourists suffer abroad, and cheap exports are snapped up by foreign countries so rapidly as to raise prices of exports at home (e.g., the American wheat-and-meat price inflation). So that American exporters might indeed benefit, but only at the expense of the inflation-ridden American consumer. The crippling uncertainty of rapid exchange rate fluctuations was brought starkly home to Americans with the rapid plunge of the dollar in foreign exchange markets in July 1973.

Since the United States went completely off gold in August 1971 and established the Friedmanite fluctuating fiat system in March 1973, the United States and the world have suffered the most intense and most sustained bout of peacetime inflation in the history of the world. It should be clear by now that this is scarcely a coincidence. Before the dollar was cut loose from gold, Keynesians and Friedmanites, each in their own way devoted to fiat paper money, confidently predicted that when fiat money was established, the market price of gold would fall promptly to its nonmonetary level, then estimated at about $8 an ounce. In their scorn of gold, both groups maintained that it was the mighty dollar that was propping up the price of gold, and not vice versa. Since 1971, the market price of gold has never been below the old fixed price of $35 an ounce, and has almost always been enormously higher. When, during the 1950s and 1960s, economists such as Jacques Rueff were calling for a gold standard at a price of $70 an ounce, the price was considered absurdly high. It is now even more absurdly low. The far higher gold price is an indication of the calamitous deterioration of the dollar since "modern" economists had their way and all gold backing was removed.

It is now all too clear that the world has become fed up with the unprecedented inflation, in the United States and throughout the world, that has been sparked by the fluctuating fiat currency era inaugurated in 1973. We are also weary of the extreme volatility and unpredictability of currency exchange rates. This volatility is the consequence of the national fiat money system, which fragmented the world's money and added artificial political instability to the natural uncertainty in the free-market price system. The Friedmanite dream of fluctuating fiat money lies in ashes, and there is an understandable yearning to return to an international money with fixed exchange rates.

Unfortunately, the classical gold standard lies forgotten, and the ultimate goal of most American and world leaders is the old Keynesian vision of a one-world fiat paper standard, a new currency unit issued by a World Reserve Bank (WRB). Whether the new currency be termed "the bancor" (offered by Keynes), the "unita" (proposed by World War II United States Treasury official Harry Dexter White), or the "phoenix" (suggested by *The Economist*) is unimportant. The vital point is that such an international paper currency, while indeed free of balance of payments crises since the WRB could issue as much bancors as it wished and supply them to its country of choice, would provide for an open channel for unlimited world-wide inflation, unchecked by either balance-of-payments crises or by declines in exchange rates. The WRB would then be the all-powerful determinant of the world's money supply and its national distribution. The WRB could and would subject the world to what it believes will be a wisely-controlled inflation. Unfortunately, there would then be nothing standing in the way of the unimaginably catastrophic economic holocaust of world-wide runaway inflation, nothing, that is, except the dubious capacity of the WRB to fine-tune the world economy.

While a world-wide paper unit and Central Bank remain the ultimate goal of world's Keynesian-oriented leaders, the more realistic and proximate goal is a return to a glorified Bretton Woods scheme, except this time without the check of any backing in gold. Already the world's major Central Banks are attempting to "coordinate" monetary and economic policies, harmonize rates of inflation, and fix exchange rates. The militant drive for a European paper currency issued by a European Central Bank seems on the verge of success. This goal is being sold to the gullible public by the fallacious claim that a free-trade European Economic Community (EEC) necessarily requires an overarching European bureaucracy, a uniformity of taxation throughout the EEC, and, in particular, a European Central Bank and paper unit. Once that is achieved, closer coordination with the Federal Reserve and other major Central Banks will follow immediately. And then, could a World Central Bank be far behind? Short of that ultimate goal, however, we may soon be plunged into yet another Bretton Woods, with all the attendant crises of the balance of payments and Gresham's Law that follow from fixed exchange rates in a world of fiat moneys.

As we face the future, the prognosis for the dollar and for the international monetary system is grim indeed. Until and unless we return to the classical gold standard at a realistic gold price, the international money system is fated to shift back and forth between fixed and fluctuating exchange rates with each system posing unsolved problems, working badly, and finally disintegrating. And fueling this disintegration will be the continued inflation of the supply of dollars and hence of American prices which show no sign of abating. The prospect for the future is accelerating and eventually runaway inflation at home, accompanied by monetary breakdown and economic warfare abroad. This prognosis can only be changed by a drastic alteration of the American and world monetary system: by the return to a free market commodity money such as gold, and by removing government totally from the monetary scene.

THE CASE FOR A 100 PERCENT
GOLD DOLLAR

PREFACE

WHEN THIS ESSAY WAS published, nearly thirty years ago, America was in the midst of the Bretton Woods system, a Keynesian international monetary system that had been foisted upon the world by the United States and British governments in 1945. The Bretton Woods system was an international dollar standard masquerading as a "gold standard," in order to lend the well-deserved prestige of the world's oldest and most stable money, gold, to the increasingly inflated and depreciated dollar. But this post-World War II system was only a grotesque parody of a gold standard. In the preWorld War I "classical" gold standard, every currency unit, be it dollar, pound, franc, or mark, was defined as a certain unit of weight of gold. Thus, the "dollar" was defined as approximately 1/20 of an ounce of gold, while the pound sterling was defined as a little less than 1/4 of a gold ounce, thus fixing the exchange rate between the two (and between all other currencies) at the ratio of their weights.[1]

---

[1]The precise ratio of gold weights amounted to defining the pound sterling as equal to $4.86656.

Since every national currency was defined as being a certain weight of gold, paper francs or dollars, or bank deposits were redeemable by the issuer, whether government or bank, in that weight of gold. In particular, these government or bank moneys were redeemable on demand in gold coin, so that the general public could use gold in everyday transactions, providing a severe check upon any temptation to over-issue. The pyramiding of paper or bank credit upon gold was therefore subject to severe limits: the ability by currency holders to redeem those liabilities in gold on demand, whether by citizens of that country or by foreigners. If, in that system, France, for example, inflated the supply of French francs (either in paper or in bank credit), pyramiding more francs on top of gold, the increased money supply and incomes in francs would drive up prices of French goods, making them less competitive in terms of foreign goods increasing French imports and pushing down French exports, with gold flowing out of France to pay for these balance of payments deficits. But the outflow of gold abroad would put increasing pressure upon the already top-heavy French banking system, even more top-heavy now that the dwindling gold base of the inverted money pyramid was forced to support and back up a greater amount of paper francs. Inevitably, facing bankruptcy, the French banking system would have to contract suddenly, driving down French prices and reversing the gold outflow.

In this way, while the classical gold standard did not prevent boom-bust cycles caused by inflation of money and bank credit, it at least kept that inflation and those cycles in close check.

The Bretton Woods system, an elaboration of the British-induced "gold exchange standard" of the 1920s, was very different. The dollar was defined at 1/35 of a gold ounce; the dollar, however, was only redeemable in large bars of gold bullion by foreign governments and central banks. Nowhere was there redeemability in gold coin; indeed, no private individual or firm could redeem in either coin or bullion. In fact, American citizens were prohibited from owning or holding gold at all, at home or abroad, beyond very small amounts permitted to coin collectors, dentists, and for industrial purposes. None of the other countries' currencies after World War II were either defined or redeemable in gold; instead, they were defined in terms of the dollar, dollars constituting the monetary reserves behind francs, pounds, and marks, and these national money supplies were in turn pyramided on top of dollars.

The result of this system was a seeming bonanza, during the 1940s and 1950s, for American policymakers. The United States was able to issue more paper and credit dollars, while experiencing only small price increases. For as the supply of dollars increased, and the United States experienced the usual balance of payments deficits of inflating countries, other countries, piling up dollar balances, would not, as before 1914, cash them in for gold. Instead, they would accumulate dollar balances and pyramid more francs, lira, etc. on top of them. Instead of each country, then, inflating its own money on top of gold and being severely limited by other countries demanding that gold, these other countries themselves inflated further on top of their increased supply of dollars. The United States was thereby able to "export inflation" to other countries, limiting its own price increases by imposing them on foreigners.

The Bretton Woods system was hailed by Establishment "macroeconomists" and financial experts as sound, noble, and destined to be eternal. The handful of genuine gold standard advocates were derided as "gold bugs," cranks and

Neanderthals. Even the small gold group was split into two parts: the majority, the Spahr group, discussed in this essay, insisted that the Bretton Woods system was right in one crucial respect: that gold was indeed worth $35 an ounce, and that therefore the United States should return to gold at that rate. Misled by the importance of sticking to fixed definitions, the Spahr group insisted on ignoring the fact that the monetary world had changed drastically since 1933, and that therefore the 1933 definition of the dollar being 1/35 of a gold ounce no longer applied to a nation that had not been on a genuine gold standard since that year.[2]

The minority of gold standard advocates during the 1960s were almost all friends and followers of the great Austrian School economist Ludwig von Mises. Mises himself, and such men as Henry Hazlitt, DeGaulle's major economic adviser Jacques Rueff, and Michael Angelo Heilperin, pointed out that, as the dollar continued to inflate, it had become absurdly undervalued at $35 an ounce. Gold was worth a great deal more in terms of dollars and other currencies, and the United States, declared the Misesians, should return to a genuine gold standard at a realistic, much higher rate. These Austrian economists were ridiculed by all other schools of economists and

---

[2]Actually, if they had been consistent in their devotion to a fixed definition, the Spahr group should have advocated a return to gold at $20 an ounce, the long-standing definition before Franklin D. Roosevelt began tampering with the gold price in 1933. The "Spahr group" consisted of two organizations: the Economists' National Committee on Monetary Policy, headed by Professor Walter E. Spahr of New York University; and an allied laymen's activist group, headed by Philip McKenna, called The Gold Standard League. Spahr expelled Henry Hazlitt from the former organization for the heresy of advocating return to gold at a far higher price (or lower weight).

financial writers for even mentioning that gold might even be worth the absurdly high price of $70 an ounce. The Misesians predicted that the Bretton Woods system would collapse, since relatively hard money countries, recognizing the continuing depreciation of the dollar, would begin to break the informal gentleman's rules of Bretton Woods and insistently demand redemption in gold that the United States did not possess.

The only other critics of Bretton Woods were the growing wing of Establishment economists, the Friedmanite monetarists. While the monetarists also saw the monetary crises that would be entailed by fixed rates in a world of varying degrees of currency inflation, they were even more scornful of gold than their rivals, the Keynesians. Both groups were committed to a fiat paper standard, but whereas the Keynesians wanted a dollar standard cloaked in a fig-leaf of gold, the monetarists wanted to discard such camouflage, abandon any international money, and simply have national fiat paper moneys freely fluctuating in relation to each other. In short, the Friedmanites were bent on abandoning all the virtues of a world money and reverting to international barter.

Keynesians and Friedmanites alike maintained that the gold bugs were dinosaurs. Whereas Mises and his followers held that gold was giving backing to paper money, both the Keynesian and Friedmanite wings of the Establishment maintained precisely the opposite: that it was sound and solid dollars that were giving value to gold. Gold, both groups asserted, was now worthless as a monetary metal. Cut dollars loose from their artificial connection to gold, they chorused in unison, and we will see that gold will fall to its nonmonetary value, then estimated at approximately $6 an ounce.

There can be no genuine laboratory experiments in human affairs, but we came as close as we ever will in 1968, and still more definitively in 1971. Here were two firm and opposing sets of predictions: the Misesians, who stated that if the dollar and gold were cut loose, the price of gold in ever-more inflated dollars would zoom upward; and the massed economic Establishment, from Friedman to Samuelson, and even including such ex-Misesians as Fritz Machlup, maintaining that the price of gold would, if cut free, plummet from $35 to $6 an ounce.

The allegedly eternal system of Bretton Woods collapsed in 1968. The gold price kept creeping above $35 an ounce in the free gold markets of London and Zurich; while the Treasury, committed to maintaining the price of gold at $35, increasingly found itself drained of gold to keep the gold price down. Individual Europeans and other foreigners realized that because of this Treasury commitment, the dollar was, for them, in essence redeemable in gold bullion at $35 an ounce. Since they saw that dollars were really worth a lot less and gold a lot more than that, these foreigners kept accelerating that redemption. Finally, in 1968, the United States and other countries agreed to scuttle much of Bretton Woods, and to establish a "two-tier" gold system. The governments and their central banks would keep the $35 redeemability among themselves as before, but they would seal themselves off hermetically from the pesky free gold market, allowing that price to rise or fall as it may. In 1971, however, the rest of the Bretton Woods system collapsed. Increasingly such hard-money countries as West Germany, France, and Switzerland, getting ever more worried about the depreciating dollar, began to break the gentlemen's rules and insist on redeeming their dollars in gold, as they had a right to do. But as soon as a substantial number of European countries were no longer content to inflate on top of depreciating dollars, and demanded gold instead, the entire system inevitably collapsed. In effect declaring national bankruptcy on August 15, 1971, President Nixon took the United States off the last shred of a gold standard and put an end to Bretton Woods.

Gold and the dollar was thus cut loose in two stages. From 1968 to 1971, governments and their central banks maintained the $35 rate among themselves, while allowing a freely-fluctuating private gold market. From 1971 on, even the fiction of $35 was abandoned.

What then of the laboratory experiment? Flouting all the predictions of the economic Establishment, there was no contest as between themselves and the Misesians: not once did the price of gold on the free market fall below $35. Indeed it kept rising steadily, and after 1971 it vaulted upward, far beyond the once seemingly absurdly high price of $70 an ounce.[3] Here was a clear-cut case where the Misesian forecasts were proven gloriously and spectacularly correct, while the Keynesian and Friedmanite predictions proved to be spectacularly wrong. What, it might well be asked, was the reaction of the Establishment, all allegedly devoted to the view that "science is prediction," and of Milton Friedman, who likes to denounce Austrians

---

[3]At one point, the price of gold reached $850, and is now lingering in the area of $350 an ounce. While gold bugs like to mope about the alleged failure of gold to rise still further, it should be noted that even this "depressed" gold price is tenfold the alleged eternally fixed rate of $35 an ounce. One side effect of the rising market price of gold was to ensure the total disappearance of the Spahr group. Thirty-five dollar gold is now not even a legal fiction; it is dead and buried, and it is safe to say that no one, of any school of thought, will want to resurrect it.

for supposedly failing empirical tests? Did he, or they, graciously acknowledge their error and hail Mises and his followers for being right? To ask that question is to answer it. To paraphrase Mencken, that sort of thing will happen the Saturday before the Tuesday before the Resurrection Morn.

After a dramatically unsuccessful and short-lived experiment in fixed exchange rates without any international money, the world has subsisted in a monetarist paradise of national fiat currencies since the spring of 1973. The combination of almost two decades of exchange rate volatility, unprecedentedly high rates of peacetime inflation, and the loss of an international money, have disillusioned the economic Establishment, and induced nostalgia for the once-acknowledged failure of Bretton Woods. One would think that the world would tire of careening back and forth between the various disadvantages of fixed exchange rates with paper money, and fluctuating rates with paper money, and return to a classical, or still better, a 100 percent, gold standard. So far, however, there is no sign of a clamor for gold. The only hope for gold on the monetary horizon, short of a runaway inflation in the United States is the search for a convertible currency in the ruined Soviet Union. It may well dawn on the Russians that their now nearly worthless ruble could be rescued by returning to a genuine gold standard, solidly backed by the large Russian stock of the monetary metal. If so, Russia, in the monetary field, might well end up, ironically, pointing to the West the way to a genuine free-market monetary system.

Two unquestioned articles of faith had been accepted by the entire economic Establishment in 1962. One was a permanent commitment to paper, and scorn for any talk of a gold standard. The other was the uncritical conviction that the American banking system, saved and bolstered by the structure of deposit insurance imposed by the federal government during the New Deal, was as firm as the rock of Gibraltar. Any hint that the American fractional-reserve banking system might be unsound or even in danger, was considered even more crackpot, and more Neanderthal, than a call for return to the gold standard. Once again, both the Keynesian and the Friedmanite wings of the Establishment were equally enthusiastic in endorsing federal deposit insurance and the FDIC (Federal Deposit Insurance Corporation), despite the supposedly fervent Friedmanite adherence to a market economy, free of controls, subsidies, or guarantees. Those of us who raised the alarm against the dangers of fractional-reserve banking were merely crying in the wilderness.

Here again, the landscape has changed drastically in the intervening decades. At first, in the mid-1980s, the fractional-reserve savings and loan banks "insured" by private deposit insurance firms, in Ohio and Maryland, collapsed from massive bank runs. But then, at the end of the 1980s, the entire S&L system went under, necessitating a bailout amounting to hundreds of billions of dollars. The problem was not simply a few banks that had engaged in unsound loans, but runs upon a large part of the S&L system. The result was admitted bankruptcy, and liquidation of the federally operated FSLIC (Federal Savings and Loan Insurance Corporation). FSLIC was precisely to savings and loan banks what the FDIC is to the commercial banking system, and if FSLIC "deposit insurance" can prove to be a hopeless chimera, so too can the long-vaunted FDIC. Indeed, the financial press is filled with stories that the FDIC might well become bankrupt without a further infusion of taxpayer funds. Whereas the "safe" level of FDIC reserves to the deposits it "insures" is alleged to be 1.5 percent, the ratio is now sinking to approximately 0.2 percent, and this is held to be cause for concern.

The important point here is a basic change that has occurred in the psychology of the market and of the public. In contrast to the naïve and unquestioning faith of yesteryear, everyone now realizes at least the possibility of collapse of the FDIC. At some point in the possibly near future, perhaps in the next recession and the next spate of bad bank loans, it might dawn upon the public that 1.5 percent is not very safe either, and that no such level can guard against the irresistible holocaust of the bank run. At that point, ignoring the usual mendacious assurances and soothing-syrup of the Establishment, the commercial banks might be plunged into their ultimate crisis. The United States authorities would then be faced with two stark choices. One would be to allow the entire banking system to collapse, along with virtually all the deposits and depositors in that system. Since, given the mind-set of American politicians, and their evident philosophy of "too big to fail," it is certain that they would be forced to embrace the second alternative: massive, hyper-inflationary printing of enough cash to pay off all the bank liabilities. The redeposit of such cash in the banking system would bring about an immediate runaway inflation and a massive flight from the dollar.

Such a future scenario, once seemingly unthinkable, is now definitely on the horizon. Perhaps realization of this plight will lead to increased interest, not only in gold, but also in a 100 percent banking system grounded upon a revalued gold stock.

In one sense, 100 percent banking is now easier to establish than it was in 1962. In my original essay, I called upon the banks to start issuing debentures of varying maturities, which could be purchased by the public and serve as productive channels for genuine savings which would neither be fraudulent nor inflationary. Instead of depositors each believing that they have a total, say, of $1 billion of deposits, while they are all laying claim to only $100 million of reserves, money would be saved and loaned to a bank for a definite term, the bank then relending these savings at an interest differential, and repaying the loan when it becomes due. This is what most people wrongly believe the commercial banks are doing now.

Since the 1960s, however, precisely this system has become widespread in the sale of certificates of deposit (CDs). Everyone is now familiar with purchasing CDs, and demand deposits can far more readily be shifted into CDs than they could have three decades ago. Furthermore, the rise of money market mutual funds (MMMF) in the late 1970s has created another readily available and widely used outlet for savings, outside the commercial banking system. These, too, are a means by which savings are being channeled into short-run credit to business, again without creating new money or generating a boom-bust cycle. Institutionally it would now be easier to shift from fractional to 100 percent reserve banking than ever before.

Unfortunately, now that conditions are riper for 100 percent gold than in several decades, there has been a defection in the ranks of many former Misesians. In a curious flight from gold characteristic of all too many economists in the twentieth century, bizarre schemes have proliferated and gained some currency: for everyone to issue his own "standard money"; for a separation of money as a unit of account from media of exchange; for a government-defined commodity index, and on and on.[4] It is particularly odd that economists who profess to be champions of a free-market economy, should go to such twists and turns to avoid facing the plain fact: that gold, that scarce and valuable market-produced metal, has always been, and will continue to be, by far the best money for human society.

Murray N. Rothbard
Las Vegas, Nevada
September, 1991

---

[4]For a critique of some of these schemes, see Murray N. Rothbard, "Aurophobia, Or: Free Banking On What Standard?", *Review of Austrian Economics* 6, no. 1 (1992); and "The Case for a Genuine Gold Dollar," in Llewellyn H. Rockwell, Jr., ed. *The Gold Standard: An Austrian Perspective* (Lexington, Mass.: Lexington Books, 1985), pp. 1–17.

1.
The Case for a 100 Percent
Gold Dollar

TO ADVOCATE THE COMPLETE, uninhibited gold standard runs the risk, in this day and age, of being classified with the dodo bird. When the Roosevelt administration took us off the gold standard in 1933, the bulk of the nation's economists opposed the move and advocated its speedy restoration. Now gold is considered an absurd anachronism, a relic of a tribal fetish. Gold indeed still retains a certain respectability in international trade; as the pre-eminent international money, gold as a medium of foreign trade can command support. But while foreign trade is important, I would rather choose the far more difficult *domestic* battleground, and argue for a genuine gold standard at home as well as abroad. Yet I shall not join the hardy band of current advocates of the gold standard, who call for a virtual restoration of the status quo *ante* 1933. Although that was a far better monetary system than what we have today, it was not, I hope to show, nearly good enough. By 1932 the gold standard had strayed so far from purity, so far from what it could and should have been, that its weakness contributed signally to its final breakdown in 1933.

2.
Money and Freedom

Economics cannot by itself establish an ethical system, although it provides a great deal of data for anyone constructing such a system—and everyone, in a sense, does so in deciding upon policy. Economists therefore have a responsibility, when advocating policy, to apprise the reader or listener of their ethical position. I do not hesitate to say that my own policy goal is the establishment of the free market, of what used to be called *laissez faire*, as broadly and as purely as possible. For this, I have many reasons, both economic and noneconomic, which I obviously cannot develop here. But I think it important to emphasize that one great desideratum in framing a monetary policy is to find one that is truly compatible with the free market in its widest and fullest sense. This is not only an ethical but also an economic tenet; for, at the very least, the economist who sees the free market working splendidly in all other fields should hesitate for a long time before dismissing it in the sphere of money.

I realize that this is not a popular position to take, even in the most conservative economic circles. Thus, in almost its first sentence, the United States Chamber of Commerce's pamphlet series on "The American Competitive Enterprise Economy" announced: "Money is what the government says it is."[1] It is almost universally believed that money, at least, cannot be free; that it must be controlled,

---

[1]Economic Research Department, Chamber of Commerce of the United States, *The Mystery of Money* (Washington, D.C.: Chamber of Commerce, 1953), p. 1.

regulated, manipulated, and created by government. Aside from the more strictly economic criticisms that I will have of this view, we should keep in mind that money, in any market economy advanced beyond the stage of primitive barter, is the nerve center of the economic system. If, therefore, the state is able to gain unquestioned control over the unit of all accounts, the state will then be in a position to dominate the entire economic system, and the whole society. It will also be able to add quietly and effectively to its own wealth and to the wealth of its favorite groups, and without incurring the wrath that taxes often invoke. The state has understood this lesson since the kings of old began repeatedly to debase the coinage.

3.
The Dollar: Independent Name or Unit of Weight?

"If you favor a free market, why in the world do you say that government should fix the price of gold?" And, "If you wish to tie the dollar to a commodity, why not a market basket of commodities instead of only gold?" These questions are often asked of the libertarian who favors a gold standard; but the very framing of the questions betrays a fundamental misconception of the nature of money and of the gold standard. For the crucial, implicit assumption of such questions—and of nearly all current thinking on the subject of money—is that "dollars" are an independent entity. If dollars are indeed properly things-in-themselves, to be bought, sold, and evaluated on the market, then it is surely true that "fixing the price of gold" in terms of dollars becomes simply an act of government intervention.

There is, of course, no question about the fact that, in the world of today, dollars are an independent entity, as are pounds of sterling, francs, marks, and escudos. If this were all, and if we simply accepted the fact of such independence and did not inquire beyond, then I would be happy to join Professors Milton Friedman, Leland Yeager, and others of the Chicago School, and call for cutting these independent national moneys loose from arbitrary exchange rates fixed by government and allowing a freely fluctuating market in foreign exchange. But the point is that I do not think that these national moneys should be independent entities. Why they should not stems from the very nature and essence of money and of the market economy.

The market economy and the modern world's system of division of labor operate as follows: a producer supplies a good or a service, selling it for money; he then uses the money to buy other goods or services that he needs. Let us then consider a hypothetical world of pure *laissez faire*, where the market functions freely and government has not infringed at all upon the monetary sphere. This system of selling goods for money would then be the only way by which an individual could acquire the money that he needed to obtain goods and services. The process would be: production → "purchase" of money → "sale" of money for goods.[2]

To those advocates of independent paper moneys who also champion the free market, I would address this simple

---

[2] A person could also receive money from producers by inheritance or other gift, but here again the ultimate giver must have been a producer. Furthermore, we may say that the recipient "produced" some intangible service— for instance, of being a son and heir—which provided the reason for the giver's contribution.

question: "Why don't you advocate the unlimited freedom of each individual to manufacture dollars?" If dollars are really and properly things-in-themselves, why not let everyone manufacture them as they manufacture wheat and baby food? It is obvious that there is indeed something peculiar about such money. For if everyone had the right to print paper dollars, everyone would print them in unlimited amounts, the costs being minuscule compared to the almost infinitely large denominations that could be printed upon the notes. Clearly, the entire monetary system would break down completely. If paper dollars are to be the "standard" money, then almost everyone would admit that government must step in and acquire compulsory monopoly of money creation so as to check its unlimited increase. There is something else wrong with everyone printing his own dollars: for then the chain from production of goods through "purchase" of money to "sale" of money for goods would be broken, and anyone could create money without having to be a producer first. He could consume without producing, and thus seize the output of the economy from the genuine producers.

Government's compulsory monopoly of dollar-creation does not solve all these problems, however, and even makes new ones. For what is there to prevent *government* from creating money at its own desired pace, and thereby benefiting itself and its favored citizens? Once again, nonproducers can create money without producing and obtain resources at the expense of the producers. Furthermore, the historical record of governments can give no one confidence that they will not do precisely that—even to the extent of hyperinflation and chaotic breakdown of the currency.

Why is it that historically, the relatively free market never had to worry about people wildly setting up money factories and printing unlimited quantities?[3] If "money" really means dollars and pounds and francs, then this would surely have been a problem. But the nub of the issue is this: On the pristine free market, money does not and cannot mean the names of paper tickets. Money means a certain commodity, previously useful for other purposes on the market, chosen over the years by that market as an especially useful and marketable commodity to serve as a medium for exchanges. No one prints dollars on the purely free market because *there are, in fact, no dollars*; there are only commodities, such as wheat, automobiles, and gold. In barter, commodities are exchanged for each other, and then, gradually, a particularly marketable commodity is increasingly used as a medium of exchange. Finally, it achieves general use as a medium and becomes a "money." I need not go through the familiar but fascinating story of how gold and silver were selected by the market after it had discarded such commodity moneys as cows, fishhooks, and iron hoes.[4] And I need also not dwell on the unique qualities possessed by gold and silver that caused the market to select them—those qualities lovingly enunciated by all the older textbooks on money: high marketability, durability, portability, recognizability, and homogeneity. Like every other commodity, the "price" of gold in terms of the commodities it can buy varies in accordance with its supply and demand. Since the demand for gold and silver was high,

---

[3]The American "wildcat bank" did not print money itself, but rather bank notes supposedly *redeemable* in money.

[4]On the process of emergence of money on the market, see the classic exposition of Carl Menger in his *Principles of Economics*, translated and edited by James Dingwall and Bert F. Hoselitz (Glencoe, Ill.: Free Press, 1950), pp. 257–85.

and since their supply was low in relation to the demand, the value of each unit in terms of other goods was high—a most useful attribute of money. This scarcity, combined with great durability, meant that the annual fluctuations of supply were necessarily small—another useful feature of a money commodity.

Commodities on the market exchange by their unit weights, and gold and silver were no exceptions. When someone sold copper to buy gold and then to buy butter, he sold *pounds* of copper for *ounces* or *grams* of gold to buy pounds of butter. On the free market, therefore, the monetary unit—the unit of the nation's accounts—naturally emerges as the unit of weight of the money commodity, for example, the silver ounce, or the gold gram.

In this monetary system emerging on the free market, no one can create money out of thin air to acquire resources from the producers. Money can only be obtained by purchasing it with one's goods or services. The only exception to this rule is gold miners, who can produce new money. But they must invest resources in finding, mining, and transporting an especially scarce commodity. Furthermore, gold miners are productively adding to the world's stock of gold for nonmonetary uses as well.

Let us indeed assume that gold has been selected as the general medium of exchange by the market, and that the unit of account is the gold gram. What will be the consequences of complete monetary freedom for each individual? What of the freedom of the individual to print his own money, which we have seen to be so disastrous in our age of fiat paper? First, let us remember that the gold gram is the monetary unit, and that such debasing names as "dollar," "franc," and "mark" do not exist and have never existed. Suppose that I decided to abandon the slow, difficult process of producing services for money, or of mining money, and instead decided to print my own? What would I print? I might manufacture a paper ticket, and print upon it "10 Rothbards." I could then proclaim the ticket as "money," and enter a store to purchase groceries with my embossed Rothbards. In the purely free market which I advocate, I or anyone else would have a perfect right to do this. And what would be the inevitable consequence? Obviously, that no one would pay attention to the Rothbards, which would be properly treated as an arrogant joke. The same would be true of any "Joneses," "Browns," or paper tickets printed by anyone else. And it should be clear that the problem is not simply that few people have ever heard of me. If General Motors tried to pay its workers in paper tickets entitled "50 GMs," the tickets would gain as little response. None of these tickets would be money, and none would be considered as anything but valueless, except perhaps a few collectors of curios. And this is why total freedom for everyone to print money would be absolutely harmless in a purely free market: no one would accept these presumptuous tickets.

Why not freely fluctuating exchange rates? Fine, let us have freely fluctuating exchange rates on our completely free market; let the Rothbards and Browns and GMs fluctuate at whatever rate they will exchange for gold or for each other. The trouble is that they would never reach this exalted state because they would never gain acceptance in exchange as moneys at all, and therefore the problem of exchange rates would never arise.

On a really free market, then, there would be freely fluctuating exchange rates, but only between genuine commodity moneys, since the paper-name moneys could never gain enough acceptance to enter the field. Specifically, since gold and silver have historically been the leading commodity moneys, gold and silver would probably both be moneys, and would exchange at freely fluctuating rates. Different groups and communities of people would pick one or the other money as their unit of accounting.[5]

---

[5]The exchange rate between gold and silver will inevitably be at or near their purchasing-power parities, in terms of the social array of goods available, and this rate would tend to be uniform throughout the world. For a brilliant exposition of the nature of the geographic purchasing power of money, and the theory of purchasing-power parity, see Ludwig von Mises, *The Theory of Money and Credit*, 2nd ed. (New Haven, Conn.: Yale University Press, 1953), pp. 170–86. Also see Chi-Yuen Wu, *An Outline of International Price Theories* (London: Routledge, 1939), pp. 233–34.

Since I am advocating a totally free market in money, what I am strictly proposing is not so much the gold standard as parallel gold and silver standards. By this, of course I do not mean bimetallism, with its arbitrarily fixed exchange rate between gold and silver, but freely fluctuating exchange rates between the two moneys. For an illuminating account of how parallel standards worked historically and how they were interfered with, see Luigi Einaudi, "The Theory of Imaginary Money from Charlemagne to the French Revolution," in Frederic C. Lane and Jelle C. Riemersma, eds., *Enterprise and Secular Change* (Homewood, Ill.: Irwin, 1953), pp. 229–61.

Professor Robert Sabatino Lopez writes, of the return of Europe to gold coinage in the mid-thirteenth century, after half a millennium:

> Florence, like most medieval states, made bimetallism and trimetallism a base of its monetary policy . . . it committed the government to the Sysiphean labor of readjusting the relations between different coins as the ratio between the different metals changes, or as one or another coin was debased. . . . Genoa, on the contrary, *in conformity with the principle of restricting state intervention as much as possible* [italics mine], did not try to enforce a fixed relation between coins of different metals. . . . Basically, the gold coinage of Genoa was not meant to integrate the silver and bullion coinages but to form an independent system. ("Back to Gold, 1251," *Economic History Review* [April 1956]: 224)

Names, therefore, whatever they may be, "Rothbard," "Jones," or even "dollar," could not have arisen as money on the free market. How, then did such names as "dollar" and "peso" originate and emerge in their own right as independent moneys? The answer is that *these names invariably originated as names for units of weight of a money commodity, either gold or silver*. In short, they began not as pure names, but as names of units of weight of particular money commodities. In the British pound sterling we have a particularly striking example of a weight derivative, for the British pound was originally just that: a pound of silver money.[6] "Dollar" began as the generally applied name of an ounce weight of silver coined in the sixteenth century by a Bohemian, Count Schlick, who lived in Joachimsthal, and the name of his highly reputed coins became "Joachimsthalers," or simply "thalers" or "dollars." And even after a lengthy process of debasement, alteration, and manipulation of these weights until they more and more became

---

On the merits of parallel standards and their superiority to bimetallism, see William Brough, *Open Mints and Free Banking* (New York: Putnam, 1898), and *The Natural Law of Money* (New York: Putnam, 1894). Brough called this system "Free Metallism." On the recent example of pure parallel standards in Saudi Arabia, down to the 1950s, see Arthur N. Young, "Saudi Arabian Currency and Finance," *Middle East Journal* (Summer 1953): 361–80.

[6]The fact that there was never an actual pound-weight coin of silver is irrelevant and does not imply that the pound was some form of "imaginary" unit of account. The pound was a pound of silver bullion, or an accumulation of a pound weight of silver coins. Cf. Einaudi, "Theory of Imaginary Money," pp. 229–30. The fundamental misconception here is to place too much emphasis on coins and not enough on bullion, an overemphasis, as we shall see presently, connected intimately with government intervention and with the long slide downward of the monetary unit from weight of gold and silver to pure name.

separated names, they still remained names of units of weight of specie until, in the United States, we went off the gold standard in 1933. In short, it is incorrect to say that, before 1933, the price of gold was fixed in terms of dollars. Instead, what happened was that the dollar was *defined* as a unit of weight, approximately 1/20 of an ounce of gold. It is not that the dollar was set equal to a certain weight of gold; it *was* that weight, just as any unit of weight, as, for example, one pound of copper *is* 16 ounces of copper, and is not simply and arbitrarily "set equal" to 16 ounces by some individual or agency.[7] The monetary unit was, therefore, always a unit of weight of a money commodity, and the names that we know now as independent moneys were names of these units of weight.[8]

---

[7]The monetary unit was not just a pure unit of weight, such as the ounce or the gram; it was a unit of weight of a certain money commodity, such as gold. The dollar was 1/20 of an ounce of *gold*, not of just any ounce. And here we find a crucial flaw in the idea of a composite-commodity money which has been overlooked: Just as we cannot call the monetary unit an "ounce" or "gram" or "pound" of several different, or composite, commodities, so the dollar cannot properly be the *name* of many different weights of many different commodities. The money commodity selected by the market was a single particular commodity, gold or silver, and therefore the *unit* of that money had to be of that commodity alone, and not of some arbitrary composite.

[8]This is why, in the older books, a discussion of money and monetary standards often takes place as part of a general discussion of weights and measures. Thus in Barnard's work on international unification of weights and measures, the problem of international unification of monetary units was discussed in an appendix, along with other appendixes on measures of capacity and metric system. Frederick A.P. Barnard, *The Metric System of Weights and Measures*, rev. ed. (New York: Columbia College, 1872).

Economists, of course, admit that our modern national moneys emerged originally from gold and silver, but they are inclined to dismiss this process as a historical accident from which we have now been happily emancipated. But Ludwig von Mises has shown, in his regression theorem, that logically money can only originate in a nonmonetary commodity, chosen gradually by the market to be an ever more general medium of exchange. Money cannot originate as a new fiat name, either by government edict or by some form of social compact. The basic reason is that the demand for money on any "day," X, which along with the supply of money determines the purchasing power of the money unit on that "day," itself depends on the very existence of a purchasing power on the previous "day," X-1. For while every other commodity on the market is useful in its own right, money (or a monetary commodity considered in its strictly *monetary* use), is only useful to *exchange* for other goods and services. Hence, alone among goods, money depends for its use and demand on having a pre-existing purchasing power. Since this is true for any "day" when money exists, we can push the logical regression backward, to see that ultimately the money commodity must have had a use in the "days" previous to money, that is, in the world of barter.[9]

---

[9]Ludwig von Mises developed the very important regression theorem in his *Theory of Money and Credit*, pp. 97–123, and defended it against the criticisms of Benjamin M. Anderson and Howard S. Ellis in his *Human Action* (New Haven, Conn.: Yale University Press, 1949), pp. 405–08. Also see Joseph A. Schumpeter, *History of Economic Analysis* (New York: Oxford University Press, 1954), p. 1090. For a reply to Professor J.C. Gilbert's contention that the establishment of the *Rentenmark* disproved the regression theorem, see Murray N. Rothbard "Toward a Reconstruction of Utility and Welfare Economics," in Mary Sennholz, ed., *On Freedom and Free Enterprise* (Princeton, N.J.: D. Van Nostrand, 1956), p. 236n.

I want to make it clear what I am *not* saying. I am not saying that fiat money, once established on the ruins of gold, cannot then continue indefinitely on its own. Unfortunately, such ultrametallists as J. Laurence Laughlin were wrong; indeed, if fiat money could not continue indefinitely, I would not have to come here to plead for its abolition.

4.

The Decline from Weight to Name: Monopolizing the Mint

The debacle of 1931–1933, when the world abandoned the gold standard, was not a sudden shift from gold weight to paper name; it was but the last step in a lengthy, complex process. It is important, not just for historical reasons but for framing public policy today, to analyze the logical steps in this transformation. Each stage of this process was caused by another act of government intervention.

On the market, commodities take different forms for different uses, and so, on a free market, would gold or silver.

The latest criticism of the regression theorem is that of Professor Patinkin, who accuses Mises of inconsistency in basing this theorem on deriving the marginal utility of money from the marginal utility of the goods that it will purchase, rather than from the marginal utility of cash holdings, the latter approach being used by Mises in the remainder of his work. Actually, the regression theorem in Mises's system is not inconsistent, but operates on a different plane, for it shows that the very marginal utility of money *to hold*—as elsewhere analyzed by Mises—is itself based upon the *prior* fact that money has a purchasing power in *goods*. Don Patinkin, *Money, Interest, and Prices* (Evanston, Ill.: Row, Peterson, 1956), pp. 71–72, 414.

The basic form of processed gold is gold bullion, and ingots
or bars of bullion would be used for very large transactions.
For smaller, everyday transactions, the gold would be
divided into smaller pieces, coins, hardened by the slight
infusion into an alloy to prevent abrasion (accounted for in
the final weight). It should be understood that all forms of
gold would really be money, since gold exchanges by weight.
A gold ornament is itself money as well as ornament; it
could be used in exchange, but it is simply not in a convenient shape for exchanges, and would probably be melted
back into bullion before being used as money. Even sacks of
gold dust might be used for exchange in mining towns. Of
course it costs resources to shift gold from one form to
another, and therefore on the market coins would tend to be
at a premium over the equivalent weight in bullion, since it
generally costs more to produce a coin out of bullion than
to melt coins back into bullion.

The first and most crucial act of government intervention in the market's money was its assumption of the
compulsory monopoly of minting—the process of transforming bullion into coin. The pretext for socialization of
minting—one which has curiously been accepted by almost
every economist—is that private minters would defraud the
public on the weight and fineness of the coins. This argument rings peculiarly hollow when we consider the long
record of governmental debasement of the coinage and of
the monetary standard. But apart from this, we certainly
know that private enterprise has been able to supply an
almost infinite number of goods requiring high precision
standards; yet nobody advocates nationalization of the
machine-tool industry or the electronics industry in order
to safeguard these standards. And no one wants to abolish
all contracts because some people might commit fraud in

making them. Surely the proper remedy for any fraud is the general law in defense of property rights.[10]

The standard argument against private coinage is that the minting business operates by a mysterious law of its own—Gresham's Law—where "bad money drives out good," in contrast to other areas of competition, where the good product drives out the bad.[11] But Mises has brilliantly shown that this formulation of Gresham's Law is a misinterpretation, and that the Law is a subdivision of the usual effects of price control by government: in this case, the government's artificial fixing of an exchange rate between two

---

[10]Presumably, on the free market private citizens will also safeguard their coins by testing their weight and purity—as they do their monetary bullion—or will mint coins with those private minters who have established reputations for probity and efficiency.

Even in the heyday of the gold standard there were few writers willing to go beyond the bounds of social habit to concede the feasibility of private minting. A notable exception was Herbert Spencer, *Social Statics* (New York: Appleton, 1890), pp. 488–89. The French economist Paul Leroy-Beaulieu also favored free private coinage. See Charles A. Conant, *The Principles of Money and Banking* (New York: Harper, 1905), vol. 1, pp. 127–28. Also see Leonard E. Read, *Government—An Ideal Concept* (Irvington-on-Hudson, N.Y.: Foundation for Economic Education, 1954), pp. 82ff. Recently Professor Milton Friedman, though completely out of sympathy with the gold standard, has, remarkably, taken a similar stand in *A Program for Monetary Stability* (New York: Fordham University Press, 1960), p. 5.

For historical examples of successful private coinage, see B.W. Barnard, "The Use of Private Tokens for Money in the United States," *Quarterly Journal of Economics* (1916–47): 617–26; Conant, vol. 1, pp. 127–32; Lysander Spooner, *A Letter to Grover Cleveland* (Boston: Tucker, 1886), p. 69; and J. Laurence Laughlin, *A New Exposition of Money, Credit and Prices* (Chicago: University of Chicago Press, 1931), vol. 1, pp. 47–51.

[11]Thus, see W. Stanley Jevons's criticism of Spencer in his *Money and the Mechanism of Exchange*, 15th ed. (London: Kegan Paul, 1905), pp. 63–66.

or more moneys creates a shortage of the artificially under-valued money and a surplus of the over-valued money. Gresham's Law is therefore a law of government intervention rather than one of the free market.[12]

The state's nationalization of the minting business injured the free market and the monetary system in many ways. One neglected point is that government minting is subject to the same flaws, inefficiencies, and tyranny over the consumer as every other government operation. Since coins are a convenient monetary shape for daily transactions, the state's decree that only X, Y, and Z denominations shall be coined imposes a loss of utility on consumers and substitutes uniformity for the diversity of the market. It also begins the long disastrous slide from an emphasis on weight to an emphasis on name, or tale. In short, under private coinage there would be a number of denominations, in strict accordance with the variety of consumer wants. The private stamp would probably guarantee fineness rather than weight, and the coins would circulate by weight. But if the government decrees just a few denominations, then weight begins to be disregarded, and the name of the coin to be considered more and more. For example, the problem persisted in Europe for centuries of what to do with old, worn coins. If a 30-gram coin was worn down to 25 grams, the simplest thing would be for the old coin to circulate *not*

---

[12]See Mises, *Human Action*, pp. 432n, 447, 754. Mises was partly anticipated at the turn of the century by William Brough:

> The more efficient money will always drive from the circulation the less efficient if the individuals who handle money are left free to act in their own interest. It is only when bad money is endorsed by the State with the property of legal tender that it can drive good money from circulation. (*Open Mints and Free Banking*, pp. 35–36)

at the old and now misleading 30 grams but at the new, correct 25 grams. The fact that the state itself had stamped 30 grams on the new coin, however, was somehow considered an insuperable barrier to such a simple solution. And, furthermore, much monetary debasement took place through the state's decree that new and old coins be treated alike, with Gresham's Law causing new coins to be hoarded and only old ones to circulate.[13]

The royal stamp on coins also gradually shifted emphasis from weight to tale by wrapping coinage in the trappings of the mystique of state "sovereignty." For many centuries it was considered no disgrace for foreign gold and silver coins to circulate in any area; monetary nationalism was yet in its infancy. The United States used foreign coins almost exclusively through the first quarter of the nineteenth century. But gradually foreign coins were outlawed, and the name of the national state's unit became enormously more significant.

Debasement through the centuries greatly spurred a loss of confidence in money as a unit of weight. There is only one point to any standard of weight: that it be eternally fixed. The international meter must always be the international meter. But using their minting monopoly, the state rulers juggled standards of monetary weight to their own economic advantage. It was as if the state were a huge warehouse that had accepted many pounds of copper or other

---

[13]The minting monopoly also permitted the state to charge a monopoly price ("seigniorage") for its minting service, which imposed a special burden on conversion from bullion to coin. In later years the state granted the subsidy of costless coinage, over-stimulating the transformation of bullion to coin. Modern adherents of the gold standard unfortunately endorse the subsidy of gratuitous coinage. Where coinage is private and marketable, the firms will of course charge a fee covering approximately the true costs of minting (such a fee is known as "brassage").

commodity from its clients, and then, when the clients came to redeem, the warehouseman suddenly announced that henceforth a pound would equal 12 ounces instead of 16, and paid out only three fourths of the copper, pocketing the other fourth for his own use. It is perhaps superfluous to point out that any private agency doing such a thing would be promptly branded as criminal.[14]

5.
The Decline from Weight to Name:
Encouraging Bank Inflation

The natural tendency of the state is inflation. This statement will shock those accustomed to viewing the state as a committee of the whole nation ardently dispensing the general welfare, but I think it nonetheless true. The reason seems to be obvious. As I have mentioned above, money is acquired on the market by producing goods and services, and then buying money in exchange for these goods. But there is another way to obtain money: creating money oneself without producing—by counterfeiting. Money creation is a much less costly method than producing; therefore the state, with its ever-tightening monopoly of money creation,

---

[14]Besides the minting monopoly, the other critical device for government control of money has been legal-tender laws, superfluous at best, mischievous and a means of arbitrary exchange-rate fixing at worst. As William Brough stated: "There is no more case for a special law to compel the receiving of money than there is for one to compel the receiving of wheat or of cotton. The common law is as adequate for the enforcement of contracts in the one case as in the other" (*The Natural Law of Money*, p. 135). The same position was taken by T.H. Farrer, *Studies in Currency, 1898* (London: Macmillan, 1898), pp. 42ff.

has a simple route that it can take to benefit its own members and its favored supporters.[15] And it is a more enticing and less disturbing route than taxes—which might provoke open opposition. Creating money, on the contrary, confers open and evident benefits on those who create and first receive it; the losses it imposes on the rest of society remain hidden to the lay observer. This tendency of the state should alone preclude all the schemes of economists and other writers for government to issue and stabilize the supply of paper money.

While countries were still on a specie standard, bank notes and government paper were issued as redeemable in specie. They were money substitutes, essentially warehouse receipts for gold, that could be redeemed in face value on demand. Soon, however, the issue of receipts went beyond 100 percent reserve to outright money creation. Governments have persistently tried their best to promote, encourage, and expand the circulation of bank and government paper, and to discourage the people's use of gold itself. Any individual bank has two great checks on its creation of money: a call for redemption by nonclients (that is, by clients of other banks, or by those who wish to use standard money), and a crisis of confidence in the bank by its clients, causing a "run." Governments have continually operated to widen these limits, which would be narrow in a system of

---

[15]This is a corollary of Franz Oppenheimer's brilliant distinction between the two basic alternate routes to wealth, production and exchange, which he called "the economic means"; and seizure or confiscation, which he called "the political means." Inflation, which I am defining here as the creation of money (i.e., an increase of money substitutes not backed 100 percent by standard specie), is thus revealed as one of the major political means. Oppenheimer defined the state, incidentally, as the organization of the political means" (*The State* [New York: Vanguard Press, 1926], pp. 24ff.).

"free banking"—a system where banks are free to do anything they please, so long as they promptly redeem their obligations to pay specie. They have created a central bank to widen the limits to the whole country by permitting all banks to inflate together—under the tutelage of the government. And they have tried to assure the banks that the government will not permit them to fail, either by coining the convenient doctrine that the central bank must be a "lender of last resort" or reserves to the banks, or, as in America, by simply "suspending specie payments," that is, by permitting banks to continue operations while refusing to redeem their contractual obligations to pay specie.[16]

---

[16]It is a commonly accepted myth that the excess of wildcat banks in America stemmed from free banking; actually a much stronger cause was the tradition, beginning in 1814 and continuing in every economic crisis thereafter, of permitting banks to continue in operation without paying in specie.

It is also a widespread myth that central banks are inaugurated in order to *check* inflation by commercial banks. The second Bank of the United States, on the contrary, was inaugurated in 1817 as an inflationist sop to the state-chartered banks, which had been permitted to run riot without paying in specie since 1814. It was a weak substitute for compelling a genuine return to specie payments. This was correctly pointed out at the time by such hard-money stalwarts as Daniel Webster and John Randolph of Roanoke. Senator William H. Wells, Federalist of Delaware, said that the Bank Bill was "ostensibly for the purpose of correcting the diseased state of our paper currency by restraining and curtailing the overissue of bank paper, and yet it came prepared to inflict upon us the same evil; being itself nothing more than simply a paper-making machine." *Annals of Congress*, 14 Cong., 1 Sess., April 1, 1816, pp. 267–70. Also see ibid., pp. 1066, 1091, 1110ff.

As for the Federal Reserve System, the major arguments for its adoption were to make the money supply more "elastic" and to centralize reserves and thus make them more "efficient," i.e., to facilitate and promote

Another device used over the years by governments was to persuade the public not to use gold in their daily transactions; to do so was scorned as an anachronism unsuited to the modern world. The yokel who didn't trust banks became a common object of ridicule. In this way, gold was more and more confined to the banks and to use for very large transactions; this made it very much easier to go off the gold standard during the Great Depression, for then the public could be persuaded that the only ones to suffer were a few selfish, antisocial, and subtly unpatriotic gold hoarders. In fact, as early as the Panic of 1819 the idea had spread that someone trying to redeem his bank note in specie, that is, to redeem his own property, was a subversive citizen trying to wreck the banks and the entire economy; and by the 1930s it was thus easy to denounce gold hoarders as virtual traitors.[17]

---

inflation. As an additional fillip, reserve requirements themselves were directly lowered at the inauguration of the Federal Reserve System. Cf. the important but totally neglected work of C.A. Phillips, T.F. McManus, and R.W. Nelson, *Banking and the Business Cycle* (New York: Macmillan, 1937), pp 21ff., and passim. Also see O.K. Burrel, "The Coming Crisis in External Convertibility in U.S. Gold," *Commercial and Financial Chronicle* (April 23, 1959): 5.

For a discussion of the historical arguments on free or central banking see Vera C. Smith, *The Rationale of Central Banking* (London: King, 1936).

[17]During the Panic the economist Condy Raguet, state senator from Philadelphia, wrote to a puzzled David Ricardo as follows:

> You state in your letter that you find it difficult to comprehend, why persons who had a right to demand coin from the Banks in payment of their notes, so long forbore to exercise it. This no doubt appears paradoxical to one who resides in a country where an act of parliament was necessary to protect a bank, but the difficulty is easily solved. The whole of our population are either stockholders of banks or in debt to them. . . . An independent man, who

And so by imposing central banking, by suspending specie payments, and by encouraging a shift among the public from gold to paper or bank deposits in their everyday transactions, the governments organized inflation, and thus an ever larger proportion of money substitutes to gold (an increasing proportion of liabilities redeemable on demand in gold, to gold itself). By the 1930s, in short, the gold standard—a shaky gold base supporting an ever greater pyramid of monetary claims—was ready to collapse at the first severe depression or wave of bank runs.[18]

---

was neither a stockholder or debtor, who would have ventured to compel the banks to do justice, would have been persecuted as an enemy of society. (Raguet to Ricardo, April 18, 1821, in David Ricardo, *Minor Papers on the Currency Question, 1809-23*, Jacob Hollander, ed. [Baltimore, Maryland: The Johns Hopkins Press, 1932], pp. 199–201)

In 1931, for example, President Hoover launched a crusade against "traitorous hoarding." The crusade consisted of the Citizens' Reconstruction Organization, headed by Colonel Frank Knox of Chicago. And Jesse Jones reports that, during the banking crisis of early 1933, Hoover was seriously contemplating invoking a forgotten wartime law making hoarding a criminal offense. Jesse H. Jones and Edward Angly, *Fifty Billion Dollars* (New York: Macmillan, 1951), p. 18. It should also be noted here that the Hoover administration's alleged devotion to retaining the gold standard is largely myth. As Hoover's Undersecretary of the Treasury has declared rather proudly: "The going off [gold] cannot be laid to Franklin Roosevelt. It had been determined to be necessary by Ogden Mills, Secretary of the Treasury, and myself as his Undersecretary, long before Franklin Roosevelt took office." Arthur A. Ballantine, *New York Herald-Tribune* (May 5, 1958) p. 18.

[18]Currently, the worst example of government aid to banks is the highly popular deposit insurance—for this means that banks have virtual carte blanche from government to protect them from any redemption crisis. As a result, virtually all natural market checks on bank inflation have been destroyed. Query: If banks are thus protected from losses by government, to what extent are they still private institutions?

6.
100 Percent Gold Banking

We have thus come to the cardinal difference between myself and the bulk of those economists who still advocate a return to the gold standard. These economists, represented by Dr. Walter E. Spahr and his associates in the Economists' National Committee on Monetary Policy, essentially believe that the old pre-1933 gold standard was a fine and viable institution in all its parts, and that going off gold in 1933 was a single wicked act of will that only needs to be repealed in order to reestablish our monetary system on a sound foundation. I, on the contrary, view 1933 as but the last link in a whole chain of unfortunate actions; it seems clear to me that the gold standard of the 1920s was so vitiated as to be ready to collapse. A return to such a gold standard, while superior to the present system, would only pave the way for another collapse—and this time, I am afraid, gold would get no further chance. Although the transition period would be more difficult, it would be kinder to the gold standard, as well as better for the long-run economic health of the country, to go back to a stronger, more viable gold standard than the one we have lost.

I daresay that my audience has been too much exposed to the teachings of the Chicago School to be shocked at the idea of 100 percent reserve banking. This topic, of course, is worthy of far more space than I can give it here. I can only say that my position on 100 percent banking differs considerably in emphasis from the Chicago School. The Chicago group basically views 100 percent money as a technique—as a useful, efficient tool for government manipulation of the money supply, unburdened by lags or friction in the banking system. My reasons for advocating 100 percent banking cut much closer to the heart of our whole system of the free market and property rights.[19] In my view, issuing promises to pay on demand in excess of the amount of goods on hand is simply fraud, and should be so considered by the legal system. For this means that a bank issues "fake" warehouse receipts—warehouse receipts, for example, for ounces of gold that do not actually exist in the vaults. This is legalized counterfeiting; this is the creation of money without the necessity for production, to compete for resources against those who have produced. In short, I believe that fractional-reserve banking is disastrous both for the morality and for the fundamental bases and institutions of the market economy.

I am familiar with the many arguments for fractional-reserve banking. There is the view that this is simply economical: The banks began with 100 percent reserves, but then they shrewdly and keenly saw that only a certain proportion of these demand liabilities were likely to be redeemed, so that it seemed safe either to lend out the gold for profit or to issue pseudo-warehouse receipts (either as bank notes or as bank deposits) for the gold, and to lend out those. The banks here take on the character of shrewd entrepreneurs. But so is an embezzler shrewd when he takes money out of the company till to invest in some ventures of his own. Like the banker, he sees an opportunity to earn a profit on *someone else's* assets. The embezzler knows, let us say, that the auditor will come on June 1 to

---

[19]The other very important difference, of course, is that I advocate 100 percent reserves in gold or silver, in contrast to the 100 percent fiat paper standard of the Chicago School. One-hundred percent gold, rather than making the monetary system more readily manageable by government, would completely expunge government intervention from the monetary system.

inspect the accounts; and he fully intends to repay the "loan" before then. Let us assume that he does; is it really true that no one has been the loser and everyone has gained? I dispute this; a theft has occurred, and that theft should be prosecuted and not condoned. Let us note that the banking advocate assumes that something has gone wrong only if everyone should decide to redeem his property, only to find that it isn't there. But I maintain that the wrong—the theft—occurs at the time the embezzler takes the money, not at the later time when his "borrowing" happens to be discovered.[20]

Another argument holds that the fact that notes and deposits are redeemable on demand is only a kind of accident; that these are merely credit transactions. The depositors or noteholders are simply lending money to the banks, which in turn act as their agents to channel the money to business firms. And why repress productive credit? Mises has shown, however, the crucial difference between a *credit transaction* and a *claim transaction*; credit always involves the purchase of a *future good* by the creditor in exchange for a present good (money). The creditor gives up a present good in exchange for an IOU for a good coming to him in the future. But a claim—and bank notes or deposits are claims to money—does not involve the creditor's relinquishing any of the present good. On the contrary the noteholder or deposit-holder still retains his money (the present good) because he has a claim to it, a warehouse receipt,

---

[20]I want to make it quite clear that I do not accuse present-day bankers of conscious fraud or embezzlement; the institution of banking has become so hallowed and venerated that we can only say that it allows for legalized fraud, probably unknown to almost all bankers. As for the original goldsmiths that began the practice, I think our opinion should be rather more harsh.

which he can redeem at any time he desires.[21] This is the nub of the problem, and this is why fractional-reserve banking creates new money while other credit agencies do not—for warehouse receipts or claims to money function on the market as equivalent to standard money itself.

To those who persist in believing that the bulk of bank deposits are really saved funds voluntarily left with the banks to invest for savers, and are not just kept as monetary cash balances, I would like to lay down this challenge: If what you say is true, why not agree to alter the banking structure to change these deposits to debentures of varying maturities? A shift from uncovered deposits to debentures will of course mean an enormous drop in the supply of money; but if these deposits are simply another form of credit, then the depositors should not object and we 100-percent theorists

---

21   It is usual to reckon the acceptance of a deposit which can be drawn upon at any time by means of note or checks as a type of credit transaction and juristically, this view is, of course, justified; but economically, the case is not one of a credit transaction. If *credit* in the economic sense means the exchange of a present good or a present service against a future good or a future service, then it is hardly possible to include the transactions in question under the conception of credit. A depositor of a sum of money who acquires in exchange for it a claim convertible into money at any time which will perform exactly the same service for him as the sum it refers to has exchanged no present good for a future good. The claim that he has acquired by his deposit is also a present good for him. The depositing of money in no way means that he has renounced immediate disposal over the utility that it commands. (Mises, *The Theory of Money and Credit*, p. 268)

What I am advocating, in brief, is a change in the juristic framework to conform to the economic realities.

will be satisfied. The purchase of a debenture will, further-more, be a genuine saving and investment of existing money, rather than an unsound increase in the money sup-ply.[22]

In sum, I am advocating that the law be changed to treat bank notes and deposits as what they are in economic and social fact: claims warehouse receipts to standard money—in short, that the note and the deposit holders be recognized as owners-in-law of the gold (or, under a fiat standard, of the paper) in the bank's vaults. Now treated in law as a debt, a deposit or note should be considered as evidence of a bailment.[23] In relation to general legal principles this

---

[22]Professor Beckhart has recently called our attention to the long-standing and successful practice of Swiss banks of issuing debentures of varying maturities, and the recent adoption of this practice in Belgium and Hol-land. While Beckhart contemplates debentures for long-term loans only, I see no reason why banks cannot issue short-term debentures as well. If business needs short-term loans, it can finance them by competing with everyone else in the market for voluntarily saved funds. Why grant the short-term market the special privilege and subsidy of creating money? Benjamin H. Beckhart, "To Finance Term Loans" (*New York Times*, May 31, 1960).

[23]   A *bailment* may be defined as the transfer of personal prop-erty to another person with the understanding that the property is to be returned when a certain purpose has been completed. . . . In a sale, we relinquish both title and pos-session. In a bailment, we merely give up temporarily the possession of the goods. (Robert O. Sklar and Benjamin W. Palmer, *Business Law* [New York: McGraw-Hill, 1942], p. 361)

Nussbaum surely begs the question when he says "Only in a broad and nontechnical sense may the relationship of the depository bank to the depositor be considered a fiduciary one. No trust proper or bailment is involved. *The contrary view would lay an unbearable burden upon banking business*" (italics mine). But if such banking business is improper, this is

would not be a radical change, since warehouse receipts are treated as bailments now. Banks would simply be treated as money warehouses in relation to their notes and deposits.[24]

---

precisely the sort of burden that should be imposed. This is but one example of what happens to jurisprudence when pragmatic considerations of "public policy" supplant the search for principles of justice. Arthur Nussbaum, *Money in the Law, National and International* (Brooklyn, N.Y.: Foundation Press, 1950), p. 105.

[24]On warehouse receipts as bailments, cf. William H. Spencer, *Casebook of Law and Business* (New York: McGraw-Hill, 1939), pp. 661ff.

Perhaps a proper legal system would also consider all "general deposit warrants" (which allow the warehouse to return any homogeneous good to the depositor) as really specific deposit warrants," which, like bills of lading, establish ownership to specific, earmarked objects.

As Jevons, noting the superiority of specific deposit warrants and realizing their relationship to money, stated:

> The most satisfactory kind of promissory document . . . is represented by bills of lading, pawn-tickets, dock-warrants, or certificates which establish ownership to a definite object. . . . The important point concerning such promissory notes is, *that they cannot possibly be issued in excess of the goods actually deposited, unless by distinct fraud* [italics mine]. The issuer ought to act purely as a warehouse-keeper, and as possession may be claimed at any time, he can never legally allow any object deposited to go out of his safe keeping until it is delivered back in exchange for the promissory note. . . . More recently a better system [than general deposit warrant] has been introduced, and each specific lot of iron has been marked and set aside to meet some particular warrant. The difference seems to be slight, but it is really very important, as opening the way to a lax fulfillment of the contract. . . . Moreover, it now [with general warrants] becomes possible to create a fictitious supply of a commodity, that is, to make people believe that a supply exists which does not exist. . . . It used to be held as a general rule of law, that any present grant or assignment of goods not in existence is without operation. (*Money and the Mechanism of Exchange*, pp. 206–12; see also p. 221)

Professor Spahr often uses the analogy of a bridge to justify fractional-reserve money. The builder of a bridge estimates approximately how many people will be using it daily. He builds the bridge on that basis and does not attempt to accommodate all the people in the city, should they all decide to cross the bridge simultaneously. But the most critical fallacy of this analogy is that the inhabitants do not then have a legal claim to cross the bridge at any time. (This would be even more evident if the bridge were owned by a private firm.) On the other hand, the holders of money substitutes most emphatically do have a legal claim to their own property at any time they choose to redeem it. The claims must then be fraudulent, since the bank could not possibly meet them all.[25]

To those who want the dollar convertible into gold but are content with the pre-1933 standard, we might cite the analysis of Amasa Walker, one of the great American economists a century ago: "So far as specie is held for the payment of these [fractional-reserve backed] notes, this kind of currency is actually convertible, and equivalent to money; but, in so far as the credit element exceeds the specie, it is only a promise to pay money, and is inconvertible. A mixed [fractional-reserve] currency, therefore can only be regarded

---

[25]A bank that fails is therefore not simply an entrepreneur whose forecasts have gone awry. It is business whose betrayal of trust has been publicly revealed. Furthermore, a rule of every business is to adjust the time structure of its assets to the time structure of its liabilities, so that its assets on hand will match its liabilities due. The only exception to this rule is a bank, which lends at certain terms of maturities, while its liabilities are all instantly payable on demand. If a bank were to match the time structure of its assets and liabilities, all its assets would also have to be instantaneous, i.e., would have to be cash.

as partially convertible; the degree of its convertibility depending upon the proportion the specie bears to the notes issued and the deposits."[26]

For a believer in free enterprise, a system of "free banking" undoubtedly has many attractions. Not only does it seem most consistent with the general institution of free enterprise, but Mises and others have shown that free banking would lead not to the infinite supply of money envisioned by such Utopian partisans of free banking as Proudhoun, Spooner, Greene, and Meulen, but rather to a much "harder" and sounder money than exists when banks are controlled by a central bank. In practice, therefore free banking would come much closer to the 100 percent ideal than the system we now have.[27] And yet if "free trade in banking is free trade in swindling," then surely the soundest course would be to take the swindling out of banking altogether. Mises's sole argument against 100 percent gold banking is that this would admit the unfortunate precedent of government control of the banking system. But if fractional-reserve banking is fraudulent, then it could be outlawed not as a form of administrative government intervention in the monetary system, but rather as part of the

---

[26]*The Science of Wealth*, 3rd ed. (Boston: Little, Brown, 1867), p. 139. In the same work, Walker presents a keen analysis of the defects and problems of a fractional-reserve currency (pp. 126–222).

[27]See Mises *Human Action*, pp. 439ff. Mises's position is that of the French economist Henri Cernuschi, who called for free banking as the best way of suppressing fiduciary bank credit: "I want to give everybody the right to issue banknotes so that nobody should take banknotes any longer" (ibid., p. 443). The German economist Otto Hübner held a similar position. See Smith, *Rationale of Central Banking*, passim.

general legal prohibition of force and fraud.[28] Within this general prohibition of fraud, my proposed banking reform would leave the private banks entirely free.[29]

7.
Objections to 100 Percent Gold

Certain standard objections have been raised against 100 percent banking and against 100 percent gold currency in particular. One generally accepted argument against any form of 100 percent banking I find particularly and strikingly curious: that under 100 percent reserves, banks would not be able to continue profitably in business. I see no reason why banks should not be able to charge their customers for their services, as do all other useful businesses. This argument points to the supposedly enormous benefits of banking; if these benefits were really so powerful, then surely the consumers would be willing to pay a service

---

[28]In short, our projected legal reform would fully comply with Mises's goal: "to place the banking business under the general rules of commercial and civil laws compelling every individual and firm to fulfill all obligations in full compliance with the terms of the contract" (*Human Action*, p. 440). Another point about free banking: to be tenable it would have to be legal for 100 percent reserve partisans to establish "Anti-Bank Vigilante Leagues," publicly calling on all note and deposit holders to redeem their obligations because their banks were really and essentially bankrupt.

[29]Cf. Walker, pp. 230–31. In *A Program for Monetary Stability*, p. 108, Milton Friedman has expressed sympathy for the idea of free banking, but oddly enough only for deposits; notes he would leave as a government monopoly. It should be clear that there is no essential economic difference between notes and deposits. They differ in technological form only; economically, they are both promises to pay on demand in a fixed amount of standard money.

charge for them, just as they pay for traveler's checks now. If they were not willing to pay the costs of the banking business as they pay the costs of all other industries useful to them, then that would demonstrate the advantages of banking to have been highly overrated. At any rate, there is no reason why banking should not take its chance in the free market with every other industry.

The major objection against 100 percent gold is that this would allegedly leave the economy with an inadequate money supply. Some economists advocate a secular increase of the supply of money in accordance with some criterion: population growth, growth of volume of trade, and the like; others wish the money supply to be adjusted to provide a stable and fixed price level. In both cases, of course, the adjusting and manipulating could only be done by government. These economists have not fully absorbed the great monetary lesson of classical economics: that the supply of money essentially does not matter. Money performs its function by being a medium of exchange; any change in its supply, therefore, will simply adjust itself in the purchasing power of the money unit, that is, in the amount of other goods that money will be able to buy. An increase in the supply of money means merely that more units of money are doing the social work of exchange and therefore that the purchasing power of each unit will decline. Because of this adjustment, money, in contrast to all other useful commodities employed in production or consumption, does not confer a social benefit when its supply increases. The only reason that increased gold mining is useful, in fact, is that the large supply of gold will satisfy more of the nonmonetary uses of the gold commodity.

There is therefore never any need for a larger supply of money (aside from the nonmonetary uses of gold or silver).

An increased supply of money can only benefit one set of people at the expense of another set, and, as we have seen, that is precisely what happens when government or the banks inflate the money supply. And that is precisely what my proposed reform is designed to eliminate. There can, incidentally, never be an actual monetary "shortage," since the very fact that the market has established and continues to use gold or silver as a monetary commodity shows that enough of it exists to be useful as a medium of exchange.

The number of people, the volume of trade, and all other alleged criteria are therefore merely arbitrary and irrelevant with respect to the supply of money. And as for the ideal of the stable price level, apart from the grave flaws of deciding on a proper index, there are two points that are generally overlooked. In the first place, the very ideal of a stable price level is open to challenge. Hoarding, as we have indicated, is always attacked; and yet it is the freely expressed and desired action on the market. People often wish to increase the real value of their cash balances, or to raise the purchasing power of each dollar. There are many reasons why they might wish to do so. Why should they not have this right, as they have other rights on the free market? And yet only by their "hoarding" taking effect through lower prices can they bring about this result. Only by demanding more cash balances and thus lowering prices can the dollars assume a higher real value. I see no reason why government manipulators should be able to deprive the consuming public of this right. Second, if people really had an overwhelming desire for a stable price level, they would negotiate all their contracts in some agreed-upon price index. The fact that such a voluntary "tabular standard" has rarely been adopted is an apt enough commentary on those stable-price-level enthusiasts who would impose their ambitions by government coercion.

Money, it is often said, should function as a yardstick, and therefore its value should be stabilized and fixed. Not its value, however, but its *weight* should be eternally fixed, as are all other weights. Its value, like all other values, should be left to the judgment, estimation, and ultimate decision of every individual consumer.[30]

---

[30]The totally neglected political theorist Isabel Paterson wrote as follows on the "compensated" or "commodity dollar" scheme of Irving Fisher, which would have juggled the weight of the dollar in order to stabilize its value:

> As all units of measure are determined arbitrarily in the first place, though not fixed by law, obviously they can be altered by law. The same length of cotton could be designated an inch one day, a foot the next, and a yard the next; the same quantity of precious metal could be denominated ten cents today and a dollar tomorrow. But the net result would be that figures used on different days would not mean the same thing; and somebody must take a heavy loss. The alleged argument for a "commodity dollar" was that a real dollar, of fixed quantity, will not always buy the same quantity of goods. Of course it will not. If there is no medium of value, no money, neither would a yard of cotton or a pound of cheese always exchange for an unvarying fixed quantity of any other goods. It was argued that a dollar ought always to buy the same quantity of and description of goods. It will not and cannot. That could occur only if the same number of dollars and the same quantities of goods of all kinds and in every kind were always in existence and in exchange and always in exactly proportionate demand; while if production and consumption were admitted, both must proceed constantly at an equal rate to offset one another. (*The God of the Machine* [New York: Putnam, 1943], p. 203n)

8.
Professor Yeager and 100 Percent Gold

One of the most important discussions of the 100 percent gold standard in recent years is by Professor Leland
Yeager.[31] Professor Yeager, while actually at the opposite
pole as an advocate of freely-fluctuating fiat moneys, recognizes the great superiority of 100 percent gold over the usual
pre-1933 type of gold standard. The main objections to the
gold standard are its vulnerability to great and sudden
deflations and the difficulties that national authorities face
when a specie drain abroad threatens domestic bank
reserves and forces contraction. With 100 percent gold, Yeager recognizes, none of these problems would exist:

> Under a 100 percent hard-money international
> gold standard, the currency of each country would
> consist exclusively of gold (or of gold plus fully-
> backed warehouse receipts for gold in the form of
> paper money and token coins). The government
> and its agencies would not have to worry about
> any drain on their reserves. The gold warehouses
> would never be embarrassed by requests to
> redeem paper money in gold, since each dollar of
> paper money in circulation would represent a dol-
> lar of gold actually in a warehouse. There would
> be no such thing as independent national mone-
> tary policies; the volume of money in each coun-
> try would be determined by market forces. The
> world's gold supply would be distributed among
> the various countries according to the demands
> for cash balances of the individuals in the various

---

[31]Leland B. Yeager, "An Evaluation of Freely-Fluctuating Exchange Rates"
(unpublished Ph.D. dissertation, Columbia University, 1952).

countries. There would be no danger of gold
deserting some countries and piling up excessively
in others, for each individual would take care not
to let his cash balance shrink or expand to a size
which he considered inappropriate in view of his
own income and wealth.

Under a 100 percent gold standard . . . the various
countries would have a common monetary system,
just as the various states of the United States now
have a common monetary system. There would be
no more reason to worry about disequilibrium in
the balance of payments of any particular country
than there is now reason to worry about disequilibrium in the balance of payments of New York
City. If each individual (and institution) took care
to avoid persistent disequilibrium in his personal
balance of payments, that would be enough. . . .
The actions of individuals in maintaining their
cash balances at appropriate levels would "auto-
matically" take care of the adequacy of each country's money supply.

The problems of national reserves, deflation, and so
forth, Yeager points out, are due to the fractional-reserve
nature of the gold standard, not to gold itself. "National
fractional reserve systems are the real source of most of the
difficulties blamed on the gold standard." With fractional
reserves, individual actions no longer suffice to assure auto-
matically the proper distribution of the supply of gold.

The difficulties arise because the mixed national
currencies—currencies which are largely paper
and only partly gold—are insufficiently international. The main defect of the historical gold
standard is the necessity of "protecting" national
gold reserves.

Central banking and its management only make
things worse:

> In short, whether a Central Bank amplifies the
> effects of gold flows, remains passive in the face
> of gold flows, or "offsets" gold flows, its behavior
> is incompatible with the principles of the full-
> fledged gold standard. . . . Indeed, any kind of
> monetary management runs counter to the prin-
> ciples of the pure gold standard.[32]

In view of this eloquent depiction of the 100 percent
gold standard, why does Yeager flatly reject it and call
instead for freely fluctuating fiat money? Largely because
only with fiat money can each governmental unit stabilize
the price level in its own area in times of depression. Now I
cannot pause to discuss further the policy of stabilization,
which I believe to be both fallacious and disastrous. I can
only point out that contrary to Professor Yeager, price
declines and exchange rate depreciation are not simple
alternatives. To believe this is to succumb to a fatal method-
ological holism and to abandon the sound path of method-
ological individualism. If, for example, a steel union in a
certain area is causing unemployment in steel by insisting
on keeping its wage rates up though prices have fallen, I
consider it at once unjust, a cause of misallocations and dis-
tortions of production, and positively futile to try to remedy
the problem by forcing all the consumers in the area to suffer by paying higher prices for their imports (through a fall
in the area's exchange rate).

One problem that every monetary statist and national-
ist has failed to face is the geographical boundary of each
money. If there should be national fluctuating fiat money,

---

[32]Ibid., pp. 9–17.

what should be the boundaries of the "nation"? Surely
political frontiers have little or no economic meaning. Professor Yeager is courageous enough to recognize this and to
push fiat money almost to a *reductio* by advocating, or at
least considering, entirely separate moneys for each region
or even locality in a nation.

Yeager has not pushed the *reductio* far enough, however.
Logically, the ultimate in freely fluctuating fiat moneys is a
different money issued by each and every individual. We
have seen that this could not come about on the free market.
But suppose that this came about by momentum from the
present system or through some other method. What then?
Then we would have a world chaos indeed, with "Rothbards," "Yeagers," "Joneses," and billions of other individual
currencies freely fluctuating on the market. I think it would
be instructive if some economist devoted himself to an
intensive analysis of what such a world would look like. I
think it safe to say that the world would be back to an enormously complex and chaotic form of barter and that trade
would be reduced to a virtual standstill. For there would no
longer be any sort of monetary medium for exchanges. Each
separate exchange would require a different "money." In
fact, since money *means* a general medium of exchanges, it
is doubtful if the very concept of *money* would any longer
apply. Certainly the indispensable economic calculation provided by the money and price system would have to cease,
since there would no longer be a common unit of account.[33]

---

[33]Professor Yeager indeed concedes that an independent money for each
person or firm would be going too far. "Beyond some admittedly indefinable point, the proliferation of separate currencies for ever smaller and
more narrowly defined territories would begin to negate the very concept
of money." But our contention is that the "indefinable point" is precisely
definable as the very first point that fiat paper enters to break up the

This is a serious and not farfetched criticism of fiat-money proposals, because all of them introduce some of this chaotic element into the world economy. In short, fluctuating fiat moneys are disintegrative of the very function of money itself. If every individual had his own money, the disintegration of the very existence of money would be complete; but national—and still more regional and local—fiat moneys already partially disintegrate the money medium. They contradict the essence of the monetary function.

Finally, Professor Yeager wonders why such "orthodox liberals" as Mises, Hayek, and Robbins should have insisted on the "monetary internationalism" of the gold standard. Without presuming to speak for them, I think the answer can be put in two parts: (1) because they favor monetary freedom rather than government management and manipulation of money, and (2) because they favored the existence of money as compared to barter—because they believed that money is one of the greatest and most significant features of the modern market economy, and indeed of civilization itself. The more general the money, the greater the scope for division of labor and for the interregional exchange of goods and services that stem from the market economy. A monetary medium is therefore critical to the free market, and the wider the use of this money, the more extensive the market and the better it can function. In short, true freedom of trade does require an international commodity money—as the history of the market economy of recent centuries has shown—gold and silver. Any breakup of such an international medium by statist fiat paper inevitably cripples and

---

world's money. See Leland B. Yeager, "Exchange Rates within a Common Market," *Social Research* (Winter 1958): 436–37.

disintegrates the free market, and robs the world of the fruits of that market. Ultimately, the issue is a stark one: we can either return to gold or we can pursue the fiat path and return to barter. It is perhaps not hyperbole to say that civilization itself is at stake in our decision.[34]

9.
The 100 Percent Gold Tradition

I therefore advocate as the soundest monetary system and the only one fully compatible with the free market and with the absence of force or fraud from any source a 100 percent gold standard. This is the only system compatible with the fullest preservation of the rights of property. It is the only system that assures the end of inflation and, with it, of the business cycle?[35] And it is the only form of gold

---

[34]Other criticisms by Yeager are really, as he recognizes at one point, criticisms of any plan for 100 percent banking, fiat or gold. There is, for example, the problem of how to suppress new forms of demand liabilities that might well arise to evade the legal restrictions. I do not think this an important argument. Fraud is always difficult to combat, and indeed continues in numerous forms to this day (as does all manner of crime). Does this mean that we should give up outlawing and punishing fraud and other crimes against person and property? Second, I am sure that the practical problems of law enforcement would be greatly reduced if the public were to receive a thorough education in the fundamentals of banking. If, in short, 100-percent-money advocates were allowed to form Anti-Bank Vigilante Leagues to point out the shakiness and immorality of fractional-reserve banking, the public would be much less inclined to evade such restrictions than it is now.

[35]*Pace* the Mises-Hayek theory of the trade cycle, which was shunted aside but not refuted by the Keynesian Revolution.

standard that fully meets the following argument of the Douglas subcommittee against a return to gold:

> An overriding reason against making gold coin freely available is that no government [or banks?] should make promises . . . which it would not be able to keep if the demand should arise. Monetary systems for over a century . . . have expanded more rapidly than would be permitted by accretions of gold.[36]

While this is undoubtedly a "radical" program for this day and age, it is important to note briefly that this program is squarely in a great tradition: not only in the economic tradition of the classical economists and the currency school, but also in the American political tradition of the Jeffersonians and the Jacksonians. In essence, this was their program. In passing it should be noted that almost all historians, with the notable exceptions of William Graham Sumner and Joseph Dorfman, have misinterpreted the Jeffersonians and Jacksonians as economically ignorant and anticapitalist agrarians lashing out at a credit system they failed to understand. Whether one agrees with their position or not, they wrote in full and sophisticated knowledge of classical economics and were fully devoted to capitalism and the free market, which they believed were hampered and not aided by the institution of fractional-reserve banking.[37] In fact, it

---

[36]*Report of the Subcommittee on Monetary, Credit, and Financial Policies of the Joint Committee on the Economic Report*, 81 Cong., 2 Sess. (Washington 1950), pp. 41ff.

[37]The conservative economic historians of the late nineteenth century saw Jackson as an ignorant agrarian trying to destroy capitalism and calling for inflation against the central bank. The progressives of the Beard school took much the same approach, except that they applauded the Jacksonians

might almost be said that these Americans were unterrified members of the currency school, lacking the almost blind devotion to the Bank of England of their more pragmatic British cousins. Indeed, the currency principle was enunciated in America several years before it made its appearance in England.[38] And such founders of the currency principle in America as Condy Raguet realized what the more eminent British tragically failed to see: that bank deposits are just as fully money substitutes as bank notes, and are therefore part of the broad money supply.[39]

After the Civil War, hard-money economists were preoccupied with battling the new greenback and free-silver problems, and the idea of 100 percent gold virtually faded

---

for their alleged anticapitalist stand. The most recent Bray Hammond-Thomas Govan school have again shifted their praise to the Whigs and the Bank of the United States, which they view as essential to a modern credit system as against the absurdly hard-money views of the Jacksonians.

[38]During the Panic of 1819, for example—several years before Thomas Joplin's enunciation of the currency principle in England—Thomas Jefferson, John Adams, John Quincy Adams, Governor Thomas Randolph of Virginia, Daniel Raymond (author of the first treatise on economics in the United States), Condy Raguet, and Amos Kendall all wrote in favor of either a pure 100 percent gold money, or of 100 percent gold backing for paper. See Murray N. Rothbard, "The Panic of 1819: Contemporary Opinion and Policy," Ph.D. dissertation (Columbia University, 1956). John Adams considered the issue of paper beyond specie as "theft," and Raymond called the practice a "stupendous fraud." Similar views were held by the important French ideologue and economist, and friend of Jefferson, Count Destutt de Tracy. Cf. Michael J.L. O'Connor, *Origins of Academic Economies in the United States* (New York: Columbia University Press, 1944), pp. 28, 38.

[39]Failure of the British currency school to realize this led to the discrediting of Peel's Act of 1844, which required 100 percent reserve for all further issue of bank notes, but left bank deposits completely free.

from view. General Amasa Walker, however, wrote into the 1860s and even he was surpassed in acumen by the brilliant and neglected writings of the Boston merchant Charles H. Carroll, who advocated 100 percent gold reserves against bank deposits as well as notes, and also urged the replacement of the name "dollar" by gold ounce or gold gram.[40] And an official of the United States Assay Office, Isaiah W. Sylvester, who has been completely neglected by historians, advocated a 100 percent dollar and parallel standards.[41] In the present century the only economist to advocate a 100 percent gold standard, to my knowledge, has been Dr. Elgin Groseclose.[42]

---

[40]On Carroll, see Lloyd W. Mints, *A History of Banking Theory* (Chicago: University of Chicago Press, 1945), pp. 129, 135ff., 155–56; and especially the collection of Carroll's writings, *Organization of Debt into Currency and Other Papers*, Edward C. Simmons, ed. (Salem, N.Y.: Ayer, 1972).

[41]Isaiah W. Sylvester, *Bullion Certificates as Currency* (New York, 1882). On parallel standards, also see Brough, *Open Mints and Free Banking*, passim. For Brough's attack on the disruption caused by independent currency names, see ibid., p. 93.

[42]Thus Groseclose:

> The practice of the goldsmiths, of using deposited funds to their own interest and profit, was essentially unsound, if not actually dishonest and fraudulent. A warehouseman, taking goods deposited with him and devoting them to his own profit, either by use or by loan to another, is guilty of a tort, a conversion of goods for which he is liable in . . . law. By a casuistry which is now elevated into an economic principle, but which has no defenders outside the realm of banking, a warehouseman who deals in money is subject to a diviner law: the banker is free to use for his private interest and profit the money left in trust . . . .
>
> Sooner or later we must abandon the pretense that we can eat our cake and have it, that we may have money on deposit ready to be withdrawn at any moment, and at the

10.
The Road Ahead

Having decided to return to a 100 percent gold dollar, we are confronted with the problem of how to go about it. There is no question about the difficulty of the transition period required to reach our goal. But once the transition

---

same time loaned out in a thousand diverse enterprises, and recognize that the only assurance of liquidity of bank deposits is to have the actual money waiting on the depositor at whatever moment he may appear. This would not mean the extinction of credit, nor the disappearance of lending institutions. But it would mean the divorcement of credit from the money mechanism, the cessation . . . of the use of credit instruments as media of exchange. . . . It would mean the disappearance of the most insidious form of fictitious credit. We could still have investment banking providing credit at long term, and bill brokers and finance companies, providing credit at short term; but such credit would not be the transfer of a fictitious purchasing power drawn from the reservoirs of a banking system whose own sources derive from the use of the bank check; the credit available would be true credit, that is, the transfer of actual, existing wealth in exchange for wealth to be created and returned at a future time. Such credit would not be inflationary, as is bank credit, for every dollar made available as purchasing power to the borrower would be the result of the abstinence from the exercise of purchasing power on the part of the lender; it would be merely the transfer of purchasing power, not the creation of purchasing power by fiction. (*Money, The Human Conflict* [Norman: University of Oklahoma Press, 1934], pp. 178, 273)

Professor F.A. Hayek, in his *Monetary Nationalism and International Stability* (New York: Longmans, Green, 1937), was highly sympathetic to 100 percent gold, and demonstrated, in some excellent analysis the superiority of 100 percent gold to the mixed, fractional-reserve gold standard, and to independent fiat moneys. In the end, he apparently set aside the proposal because of the difficulties of bank evasion; moreover, he concluded, rather inconsistently, by considering the ideal monetary system as

period is concluded, we will have the satisfaction of possessing the best monetary system known to man and of eliminating inflation, business cycles, and the uneconomic and immoral practice of people acquiring money at the expense of producers. Since we have many times the number of dollars as we have gold dollars at the present fixed weight of the dollar, we have essentially two alternative, polar routes toward 100 percent gold: either to force a deflation of the supply of dollars down to the currently valued gold stock, or to "raise the price of gold" (to lower the definition of the dollar's weight) to make the total stock of gold dollars 100 percent equal to the total supply of dollars in the society. Or we can choose some combination of the two routes.

Professor Spahr and his associates wish to return to the gold standard (though not to 100 percent gold) at the current "price" of $35 an ounce, stressing the importance of fixity of the weight of the dollar. If these were before 1933 and we were still on a gold standard, even if a defective one, I would unhesitatingly agree. The principle of a fixed weight for the dollar, and above all the principle of the sanctity of

---

directed by an international central bank, with the gold standard as only second best. Robbins, while discussing 100 percent money, was more sympathetic to free banking under a gold standard. Lionel Robbins, *Economic Planning and International Order* (London: Macmillan, 1937) pp. 269–305. In recent years, Hayek has abandoned the gold standard completely on behalf of a composite-commodity standard: "A Commodity Reserve Currency," in his *Individualism and Economic Order* (Chicago: University of Chicago Press, 1945), pp. 209–19. Since Hayek's major reason for the shift is that the total supply of gold is not flexible enough to change when demanded (and since, even in his earlier work Hayek wrote of a "rationally" determined total supply of world money, regulated by an international monetary authority), it is clear that Hayek does not see that no specific total supply of money is better than any other, and that therefore no government manipulation of the supply is desirable.

contract, are essential to our entire system of private property, and therefore would have been well worth the difficulties of a severe deflation. Aside from that, we have built
deflation into an absurd ogre, and have overlooked the
healthy consequences of a deflationary purgation of the
malinvestments of the boom, as well as the overdue aid that
fixed income groups, hit by decades of inflationary erosion,
would at last obtain from a considerable fall in prices. A
sharp deflation would also help to break up the powerful
aggregations of monopoly unionism, which are potentially
so destructive of the market economy. At any rate, while the
deflation would be nominally sharp, to the extent that people would wish to save much of their present cash holdings,
they would increase voluntary savings by purchasing bank
debentures in lieu of their deposits, thereby fostering "economic growth" and mitigating the rigors of the deflation.

On the other hand, there is no particular reason to be
devoted to the $35 figure at the present time, since the exist-
ing "gold standard" and definition of the dollar are only
applicable to foreign governments and central banks; as far
as the people are concerned, we are now on a virtual fiat
standard. Therefore, we may change the definition of the
dollar as a preliminary step to return to a full gold standard,
and we would not really be disturbing the principle of fixity.
As in the case of any definition of weight, the *initial* definition is purely arbitrary, and we are so close now to a fiat
standard that we may consider any dollar in a new standard
as an initial definition.

Depending on how we define the money supply—and I
would define it very broadly as all claims to dollars at fixed
par value—a rise in the gold price sufficient to bring the
gold stock to 100 percent of total dollars would require a
ten- to twentyfold increase. This of course would bring an
enormous windfall gain to the gold miners, but this does

not concern us. I do not believe that we should refuse an offer of a mass entry into Heaven simply because the manufacturers of harps and angels' wings would enjoy a windfall gain. But certainly a matter for genuine concern would be the enormous impetus such a change would give for several years to the mining of gold, as well as the disruption it would cause in the pattern of international trade.

Which course we take, or which particular blend of the two, is a matter for detailed study by economists. Obviously little or none of this needed study has been undertaken. I therefore do not propose here a detailed blueprint. I would like to see all of those who have become convinced of the need for a 100 percent gold standard join in such a study of the best path to take toward such a goal under present conditions. Broadly, the desired program may be summarized as follows:

1. Arrival of a 100 percent gold dollar, either by deflation of dollars to a gold stock valued at $35 per ounce, or by revaluation of the dollar at a "gold price" high enough to make the gold stock 100 percent of the present supply of dollars, or a blend of the two routes.

2. Getting the gold stock out of the hands of the government and into the hands of the banks and the people, with the concomitant liquidation of the Federal Reserve System, and a legal 100 percent requirement for all demand claims.

3. The transfer of all note-issue functions from the Treasury and the Federal Reserve to the private banks. All banks, in short, would be allowed to issue deposits *or* notes at the discretion of their clients.

4. Freeing silver bullion and its representative in silver certificates (which would now be issued by the banks) from any fixed value in gold. In short, silver ounces and their warehouse receipts would fluctuate, as do all other commodities, on the market in terms of gold or dollars, thus giving us "parallel" gold and silver moneys, with gold dollars presumably remaining the chief money as the unit of account.

5. The eventual elimination of the term "dollar," using only terms of weight such as "gold gram" or "gold ounce."[43] The ultimate goal would be the return to gold by every nation, at 100 percent of its particular currency, and the subsequent blending of all these national currencies into one unified world gold-gram unit. This was one of the considered goals at the abortive international monetary conferences of the late nineteenth century.[44] In such a world, there would be no exchange rates except between gold and silver, for the national currency names would be abandoned for

---

[43]For an eloquent plea for using pure units of weight for money instead of national names, see Jean-Baptiste Say, *A Treatise on Political Economy*, New American ed. (Philadelphia: Grigg and Elliot, 1841), pp. 256ff. Say also favored a freely fluctuating market between gold and silver.

More recently, Everett R. Taylor has advocated private coinage of gold and silver, and a 100 percent gold dollar, while another writer, Oscar B. Johannsen, has favored private coinage and free banking under a gold standard. Taylor, *Progress Report on a New Bill of Rights* (Diablo, Calif.: privately published, 1954); Johannsen, "Advocates Unrestricted Private Control Over Money and Banking," *Commercial and Financial Chronicle* (June 12, 1958): 2622ff.

[44]See Barnard, *Metric System of Weights and Measures*, and Henry B. Russell, *International Monetary Conferences* (New York: Harper, 1898), p. 61.

simple weights of gold, and all the world's money would at long last be freed from government intervention.

6. Free (but presumably not gratuitous) private coinage of gold and silver.

I must here differ with Professor Mises's and Henry Hazlitt's suggestion for return to the gold standard by first establishing a "free market" in gold by cutting the dollar completely loose from gold, and then seeing, after several years, what gold price the market would establish.[45] In the first place, this would cut the last tenuous link that the dollar still has to gold and yield us a totally fiat money. Second, the market would hardly be a "free" one, since almost all the nation's gold would be sequestered in government hands. I think it important to move in the reverse direction. The Federal government, after all, seized the people's gold in 1933 under the guise of a temporary emergency. It is important, for moral and economic reasons, to permit the people to reclaim their gold as rapidly as possible. And since the gold is still held as hostage for our dollars, I believe that the official link and official convertibility between dollars and gold should be reestablished as soon as Congress can be so persuaded. And finally, since the dollar is merely a weight of gold, properly speaking, it is not at all appropriate to establish a "market" between dollars and gold, any more than there should be a "market" between one-dollar bills and five-dollar bills.

There is no gainsaying the fact that this suggested program will strike most people as impossibly "radical" and

---

[45]Mises, *The Theory of Money and Credit*, pt. 4; and Henry Hazlitt, "Return to Gold," *Newsweek* (1954).

"unrealistic"; any suggestion for changing the status quo, no matter how slight, can always be considered by someone as too radical, so that the only thoroughgoing escape from the charge of impracticality is never to advocate any change whatever in existing conditions. But to take this approach is to abandon human reason, and to drift in animal- or plant-like manner with the tide of events. As Professor Philbrook pointed out in a brilliant article some years ago, we must frame our policy convictions on what we believe the best course to be and then try to convince others of this goal, and not include within our policy conclusions estimates of what other people may find acceptable.[46] For *someone* must propagate the truth in society, as opposed to what is politically expedient. If scholars and intellectuals fail to do so, if they fail to expound their convictions of what they believe the correct course to be, they are abandoning truth, and therefore abandoning their very *raison d'être*. All hope of social progress would then be gone, for no new ideas would ever be advanced nor effort expended to convince others of their validity.

---

[46]Clarence Philbrook, "'Realism' in Policy Espousal," *American Economic Review* (December 1953): 846–59.

INDEX

About the Author

Murray N. Rothbard (1926–1995) was the S.J. Hall distinguished professor of economics at the University of Nevada, Las Vegas, and dean of the Austrian School. He served as vice president for academic affairs at the Ludwig von Mises Institute, and editor of the *Review of Austrian Economics*, among many other journals and publications.

Professor Rothbard received his B.S., M.A., and Ph.D. from Columbia University, where he studied under Joseph Dorfman. For more than ten years, he also attended Ludwig von Mises's seminar at New York University.

Professor Rothbard is the author of thousands of articles, and his 17 books include: *The Panic of 1819*; *Man, Economy, and State*; *America's Great Depression*; *The Mystery of Banking*; *For a New Liberty*; *The Ethics of Liberty*; the four-volume *Conceived in Liberty*; and the two-volume *An Austrian Perspective on the History of Economic Thought*.